Twelfth Edition

Michigan
NOTARY PRIMER

The NNA's Handbook
for Michigan Notaries

NATIONAL NOTARY ASSOCIATION

Published by:

National Notary Association
9350 De Soto Avenue
Chatsworth, CA 91311-4926
Telephone: (800) 876-6827
Fax: (818) 700-0920
Website: NationalNotary.org
Email: nna@NationalNotary.org

©2019 National Notary Association
ALL RIGHTS RESERVED. No part of this book may be reproduced in any form without permission in writing from the publisher.

The information in this *Primer* is correct and current at the time of its publication, although new laws, regulations and rulings may subsequently affect the validity of certain sections. This information is provided to aid comprehension of state Notary Public requirements and should not be construed as legal advice. Please consult an attorney for inquiries relating to legal matters.

Twelfth Edition ©2019
First Edition ©1997

ISBN: 978-1-59767-264-1

Table of Contents

Introduction 1

The Notary Commission.. 3

Screening the Signer.. 9

Reviewing the Document... 16

Official Notary Acts 25

Recordkeeping... 39

Notary Certificate and Seal.. 43

Electronic and Remote Online Notarizations 48

Misconduct, Fines and Penalties.. 52

Michigan Laws Pertaining to Notaries Public................................. 58

About the NNA 83

Index 84

Have a Tough Notary Question?
If you were a National Notary Association member, you could get the answer to that difficult question. Join the NNA® and your membership includes access to the NNA® Hotline* and live Notary experts providing the latest Notary information regarding laws, rules and regulations.

Hours
Monday – Friday   5:00 a.m.–7:00 p.m. (PT)
Saturdays   5:00 a.m.–5:00 p.m. (PT)

NNA® Hotline Toll-Free Phone Number: 1-888-876-0827

After hours you can leave a message or email our experts at Hotline@NationalNotary.org and they will respond the next business day.

*Access to the NNA® Hotline is for National Notary Association members and NNA® Hotline subscribers only. Call and become a member today.

Introduction

You are to be commended on your interest in Michigan Notary law! Purchasing the *Michigan Notary Primer* identifies you as a conscientious professional who takes your official responsibilities seriously.

In few fields is the expression "more to it than meets the eye" truer than in Notary law. What often appears on the surface to be a simple procedure may, in fact, have important legal considerations.

The purpose of the *Michigan Notary Primer* is to provide you with a resource to help decipher the many intricate laws that affect notarization. In doing so, the *Primer* will acquaint you with all important aspects of Michigan's Notary law and with prudent notarial practices in general.

The *Michigan Notary Primer* takes you through the myriad of Notary laws and puts them in easy-to-understand terms. Every section of the law is analyzed and explained, as well as topics not covered by Michigan law but nonetheless of vital concern to you as a Notary.

For your convenience, we have reprinted the complete text of the laws of Michigan that relate to Notaries Public.

Whether you're about to be commissioned for the first time or a longtime Notary, we're sure the *Michigan Notary Primer* will provide you with new insight and understanding. Your improved comprehension of Michigan's Notary law will naturally result in your greater competence as a professional Notary Public.

Milton G. Valera
Chairman
National Notary Association

Notary Laws Explained

In layperson's language, this chapter discusses and clarifies pertinent sections of the Michigan Compiled Laws (MCL) that regulate Notaries Public. The statutes are reprinted in full in "Michigan Laws Pertaining to Notaries Public," beginning on page 58.

Additional information about Michigan's requirements for Notaries Public is available on the Secretary of State's website. For both the current application form and step-by-step instructions on the commission application process, applicants also may go to NationalNotary.org.

The Notary Commission

Application for New Commission

Qualifications. To become a first-time Notary in Michigan, or to renew a commission, the applicant (MCL 55.271[1][a]-[d]):

1) Must be at least 18 years old.

2) Must be a resident of or must maintain a principal place of business in the Michigan county in which the applicant seeks an appointment.

3) Must be able to read and write the English language.

4) Must be free of felony convictions within the past 10 years and of certain misdemeanor convictions within specified time periods that depend on the applicant's commission status.

A person who is serving a term of imprisonment in a state or federal facility is not eligible to become a Michigan Notary (MCL 55.269[3]).

Citizenship. U.S. citizenship is not required to become a Michigan Notary, though any noncitizen applicant must be a permanent legal resident. A 1984 Supreme Court decision, *Bernal v. Fainter*, declared that no state may deny a Notary commission merely on the basis of lack of U.S. citizenship.

Application. Applicants for a Michgan Notary commission must complete the approved application form, which is required by law to contain certain information (MCL 55.275[1]). The current application form is available on the Secretary of State's website.

Application Fee. A nonrefundable application fee of $10 must be submitted with the application (MCL 55.275[2]). An additional fee will required at the time of filing the official oath of office and bond with the county clerk (see page 5).

The Secretary will automatically cancel the Notary Public commission of any person who makes, draws, utters or delivers any check, draft or order of payment of a processing fee that is not honored by the bank, financial institution or other depository expected to render payment upon its first presentation (MCL 55.279[4]).

Nonresident Applicants. In addition to the application requirements for residents, nonresident applicants must indicate that they maintain a principal place of business in the county where they are requesting appointment. Such applicants must also demonstrate that their business activity will require them to perform notarial acts (MCL 55.271[e]).

Michigan Department of State. For the applicant's convenience, contact information for the Department is as follows:

>Michigan Department of State
>Office of the Great Seal
>7064 Crowner Drive
>Lansing, MI 48918
>Telephone: (517) 335-8656
>michigan.gov/sos

Notification of Appointment

Notification by Secretary of State. After approval of the application, the Secretary of State will mail the certificate of appointment as a Notary Public directly to the applicant. The certificate of appointment will identify the person as a Notary Public of the State of Michigan and will specify the term and county of the new Notary's commission (MCL 55.275[4]).

Application for Reappointment

Reappointment. A Notary seeking reappointment must apply for a new commission and follow the same procedures as when applying for a commission for the first time. To avoid a lapse in notarial powers, a Notary may submit an application for another term in advance, but no earlier than 60 days prior to expiration of the current appointment (MCL 55.279[2]).

Notary Bond

Requirement. Within 90 days before submitting an application for a Notary Public appointment, Michigan Notaries are required to obtain a $10,000 bond and file it at the office of the clerk in the county of residence (or, in the case of out-of-state applicants, the county of employment). The commission will not be issued to the applicant until the bond has been filed (MCL 55.271[1][f] and 55.273[1-2]).

Surety. The surety for the Notary's bond must be a company licensed to issue bonds in the state (MCL 55.273[2]).

Fee. The county clerk will charge at least a $10 fee to file and record the Notary's oath and bond. After the fee is paid, the county clerk will give a bond and oath certificate to the applicant.

A county with a population of more than two million may impose a fee different from the amount cited above (MCL 55.273[3]).

Protects Public. The Notary surety bond protects the public from a Notary's misconduct or negligence; it does *not* protect the Notary. Up to the coverage limit, the bond provides reimbursement for damages to anyone who suffers financially due to an improper official act on the part of the Notary (MCL 55.273[2]).

Liable for All Damages. Both the Notary and surety company may be sued for damages resulting from notarial misconduct. The surety is liable only up to the amount of the bond, but the Notary may be found liable for any amount of money for damages deemed to have been caused by the Notary's improper acts. The surety will seek compensation from the Notary for any damages it has to pay out on the Notary's behalf.

Liability. As ministerial officials, Notaries generally may be held financially responsible for any and all damages caused by their mistakes or misconduct in performing notarial acts.

If a person is financially injured by a Notary's negligence or willful failure to properly perform a notarial act — whether intentional or unintentional — the Notary may be sued in civil court and ordered to pay all resulting damages, including attorneys' fees.

A person need not be named in a document to sue a Notary for damages resulting from the Notary's handling of that document. If, for example, a lender accepts a forged, notarized deed as collateral for a loan, the lender might sue to recover losses from the Notary who witnessed the bogus deed.

Errors and Omissions Insurance. Notaries may choose to purchase insurance to cover any unintentional errors or omissions they may make. Notary errors and omissions insurance provides protection for Notaries who are involved in claims or sued for damages resulting from unintentional notarial errors and omissions. In the event of a claim or civil lawsuit, the insurance company will provide and pay for the Notary's legal counsel and absorb any damages levied by a court or agreed to in a settlement, up to the policy coverage limit. Generally, errors and omissions insurance does not cover the Notary for dishonest, fraudulent or criminal acts or omissions, or for willful or intentional disregard of the law.

Oath of Office

Requirement. Within 90 days before submitting an application for a Notary Public appointment, Michigan Notaries are required to take and file an oath of office at the office of the clerk of the county in which the Notary seeks to be appointed. The clerk will administer the required oath, in which the applicant swears to faithfully and honestly discharge the duties of the office of Notary Public for Michigan (MCL 55.273[1]).

Fee. The county clerk will charge at least a $10 fee to file and record the Notary's oath and bond. After the fee is paid, the county clerk will give a bond and oath certificate to the applicant.

A county with a population of more than two million may impose a fee different from the amount cited above (MCL 55.273[3]).

Jurisdiction

Statewide. Michigan Notaries may perform official acts throughout the state of Michigan but not beyond the state borders. They are not limited to just the respective counties in which they live (MCL 55.269[2]).

However, a Notary must reside or be employed in the county in which he or she has been appointed. If notarization takes place in a county other than the county in which the Notary is appointed, the Notary must add the completed words "Acting in the County of _____" to the certificate (MCL 55.287[2][d]).

The Notary may not witness a signing outside of Michigan and then return to the state to perform the notarization. All parts of a given notarization must be performed at the same time and place within the state of Michigan.

Michigan Notaries may notarize documents originating in another state or nation, as long as the requested notarial act complies with Michigan law. In such cases, they should ensure that the venue — the place of notarization — is correctly written on the certificate.

Term of Office

Six to Seven-Year Term. The term of office for a Michigan Notary Public is six to seven years, depending on the Notary's birthday. Each term begins with the date specified by the Department of State and ends on the Notary's birthday, not less than six years or more than seven years after the appointment, unless the appointment is officially canceled, suspended or revoked by the state (MCL 55.269[2]).

Resignation

Notification. To resign, the National Notary Association recommends that a Notary submit a written notice to the Department of State, giving an effective date. Such a resignation is appropriate if the Notary moves out of the state. The notice should be sent by certified mail.

A copy of the resignation notice may also be sent to the office of the county clerk where the Notary has filed the oath and bond.

Disposition of Seal and Records. If the resigning Notary has a seal of office or a stamp that he or she used to affix information on certificates, these should be destroyed or defaced to prevent fraudulent use. If the Notary maintained a journal of notarial acts or other recordbook, the National Notary Association recommends that the Notary retain and safeguard the records until passage of the pertinent statute of limitations.

Death of Notary

Notification. If a Notary should die, the Notary's personal representative should notify the Department of State. The notification should include the Notary's name and appointment number, as well as any additional pertinent information, and should be sent by certified mail.

Disposition of Seal and Records. If the deceased Notary has a seal of office or a stamp that he or she used to affix information on certificates, these should be destroyed or defaced to prevent fraudulent use. If the Notary maintained a journal or other recordbook, the National Notary Association recommends that the Notary's personal representative retain the journal in keeping with the pertinent statute of limitations.

Change of Address

Notification Required. If there is a change in the Notary's residence or business address, the Notary must immediately apply to the Secretary of State for a corrected Notary commission (MCL 55.281[1]).

Change of Name

Notification. When a Notary changes name, he or she must immediately apply to the Secretary of State for a corrected Notary commission (MCL 55.281[1]). ■

Screening the Signer

Personal Appearance

Requirement. The principal signer must personally appear before the Notary at the time of the notarization. This means that the Notary and the signer must both be physically present, face to face in the same room, when the notarization takes place. Notarizations may never be performed over the telephone.

Willingness

Confirmation. The Notary should make every effort to confirm that the signer is acting willingly.

To confirm willingness, the Notary need only ask signers if they are signing of their own free will. If a signer does or says anything that makes the Notary think the signer is being pressured to sign, the Notary should refuse to notarize.

Awareness

Confirmation. The Notary should make every effort to confirm that the signer is generally aware of what is taking place.

To confirm awareness, the Notary simply makes a layperson's judgment about the signer's ability to understand what is happening. A signer who cannot respond intelligibly in a simple conversation with the Notary should not be considered sufficiently aware to sign at that moment. If the notarization is taking place in a medical environment, the signer's doctor can be consulted for a professional opinion. Otherwise, if the signer's awareness is in doubt, the Notary should refuse to notarize.

Foreign-Speaking Signers. There always should be direct communication between the Notary and signer — whether

English or any other language. The Notary should never rely on an intermediary or interpreter to determine a signer's willingness or awareness. A third party may have a motive for misrepresenting the circumstances to the Notary and/or signer.

Identifying Document Signers

Three Identification Methods. In notarizing a signature on any document, Michigan law requires the Notary to identify the document signer. The following three methods of identification are acceptable (MCL 55.285):

1) The Notary's *personal knowledge* of the signer's identity (see "Personal Knowledge of Identity," below);

2) The oath or affirmation of a personally known *credible identifying witness* (see "Credible Identifying Witness," page 11); or

3) Reliable *identification documents* or ID cards (see "Identification Documents," pages 12–13).

The latter two methods of identification — credible witnesses and identification documents — are regarded as "satisfactory evidence" of identity.

Personal Knowledge of Identity

The safest and most reliable method of identifying a signer is for the Notary to depend on his or her own personal knowledge of the signer's identity. Personal knowledge means familiarity with an individual resulting from interactions with that person over a period of time sufficient to eliminate every reasonable doubt that the person has the identity claimed. The familiarity should come from association with the individual in relation to other people and should be based upon a chain of circumstances surrounding the individual.

Michigan law does not specify how long a Notary must be acquainted with an individual before personal knowledge of identity may be claimed, so the Notary's common sense must prevail. In general, the longer the Notary is acquainted with a person, and the more random interactions the Notary has had with that person, the more likely the individual is indeed personally known.

For instance, the Notary might safely regard a friend since childhood as personally known, but would be foolish to consider a person met for the first time the previous day as such. Whenever the Notary has a reasonable doubt about a signer's identity, that individual should be considered not personally known, and the identification should be made through either a credible identifying witness or reliable identification documents.

Credible Identifying Witness

Purpose. When a signer is not personally known to the Notary and is not able to present reliable ID cards, that signer may be identified on the oath (or affirmation) of a credible identifying witness (MCL 55.285[6][b]).

Qualifications. Every credible identifying witness should personally know the signer. The credible identifying witness should also be personally known by the Notary. This establishes a "chain of personal knowledge" from the Notary to the credible identifying witness to the signer. In a sense, a credible identifying witness is a walking, talking ID card.

Credible identifying witnesses must never themselves be identified to the Notary through ID cards. Any credible identifying witness should have a reputation for honesty; the witness should be a competent, independent individual who won't be tricked, cajoled, bullied or otherwise influenced into identifying someone he or she does not really know. In addition, the witness should have no direct personal interest in the transaction requiring a notarial act.

Oath (or Affirmation) for Credible Identifying Witness. To ensure truthfulness, the Notary must administer an oath or affirmation to each credible identifying witness.

If not otherwise prescribed by Michigan law, an acceptable credible-witness oath or affirmation might be:

> Do you solemnly swear that you know that the signer is the person he/she claims to be, so help you God?
>
> (Do you solemnly affirm that you know that the signer is the person he/she claims to be?)

Signature in Notary's Journal. If the Notary maintains a journal — although a journal is not required by Michigan law — each credible identifying witness should sign the Notary's journal, along with the signer. The Notary should also print each witness's name and address.

MICHIGAN NOTARY PRIMER

Not a Subscribing Witness. Notaries must not confuse credible witnesses with subscribing witnesses. (See "Proof of Execution by Subscribing Witness," pages 34–35.)

Identification Documents (ID Cards)

Acceptable Identification Documents. Michigan Notaries are allowed to use a current license, identification card or record issued by a federal or state government and containing the person's photograph and signature to identify signers whom they do not personally know (MCL 55.285[6][c]).

The best ID cards have an additional component: a physical description (e.g., "brown hair, green eyes," etc.) of the bearer. Such ID cards are considered to be "satisfactory evidence" of identity in lieu of personal knowledge, just as is the sworn word of a personally known credible identifying witness (Public Act 238 of '03, Sect. 25[6]).

Acceptable forms of identification include:

- Michigan driver's license or official nondriver's ID.

- U.S. and foreign passports.

- U.S. military ID.

- Permanent resident card, or "green card," issued by the U.S. Citizenship and Immigration Services (USCIS).

Multiple Identification. While one good identification document or card may be sufficient to identify a signer, the Notary is encouraged to ask for more.

Unacceptable Identification Documents. Unacceptable ID cards for identifying signers include Social Security cards, credit cards and birth certificates. Acceptable IDs must be current, government-issued and bear both a photograph and signature.

Name Variations. The Notary must make sure that the name on the document is the same as the name appearing on the identification presented. In certain circumstances, it may be acceptable for the name on the document to be an abbreviated form of the name on the ID — for example, John D. Smith instead of John David Smith. Last names or surnames, however, should always be the same.

Fraudulent Identification. Identification documents are the least secure of the three methods of identifying a signer, because phony ID cards are common. The Notary should scrutinize each card for evidence of tampering or counterfeiting, or for evidence that it is a genuine card that has been issued to an impostor.

Some clues that an ID card may have been fraudulently altered with include: mismatched type styles, a photograph with a raised surface, a signature that does not match the signature on the document and unauthorized lamination of the card. Smudges, erasures, smears and discolorations may also be clues.

Possible tip-offs to a counterfeit ID card include: misspelled words, a seemingly brand new card with an old date of issuance, two cards with exactly the same photograph showing the bearer in identical clothing or with an identical background and inappropriate patterns and features.

Indications that an identification card may have been issued to an impostor include the birthdate or address on the card being unfamiliar to the bearer or the ID cards seeming brand new.

Signature by Mark

Mark Serves as Signature. A person who cannot sign his or her name because of illiteracy or a physical disability may instead use a mark — an "X," for example — as a signature, as long as there are two witnesses to the making of the mark.

Witnesses. For a signature by mark to be notarized, there must be two witnesses to the making of the mark. Although a Michigan Notary is permitted to witness and notarize the same document, ideally, the Notary should not do so.

Both witnesses should sign the document and the Notary's journal. As shown below, one witness should print legibly the marker's name beside the mark on the document. It is recommended that a mark also be affixed in the Notary's journal.

In the presence of: _____
    Jane Doe
      his mark
      X
     JOHN JONES

Notarization Procedures. Because a properly witnessed mark is considered a signature under custom and law, no special Notary certificate is required. As required of any other signer, the marker must be positively identified.

Disabled Signers

Notary as Proxy Signer. A Notary may sign any document on behalf of a signer who, due to physical disability, cannot execute a document without assistance (MCL 55.293).

Direction by Signer. The Notary must be directed to sign by the person by oral, written, electronic or mechanical means — such as an electronic communication device for persons unable to speak (MCL 55.293).

Personal Appearance Required. As with other types of notarization, an individual seeking assistance with signing a document must be in the physical presence of the Notary when the Notary signs on his or her behalf (MCL 55.293).

Required Information. In addition to the usual required Notary certificate information, the Notary must inscribe beneath the signature he or she made on behalf of the signer, "Signature affixed pursuant to section 33 of the Michigan Notary Public Act," (MCL 55.293).

Notarizing for Minors

Under Age 18. Generally, persons must reach the age of majority before they can handle their own legal affairs and sign documents for themselves. In Michigan, the age of majority is 18. Normally, natural guardians (parents) or court-appointed guardians will sign on a minor's behalf. In certain cases, where minors are engaged in business transactions or serving as court witnesses, they may lawfully sign documents on their own behalf and have their signatures notarized.

Include Age Next to Signature. When notarizing for a minor, the Notary should ask the young signer to write his or her age next to the signature to alert any person relying on the document that the signer is a minor. The Notary is not required to verify the minor signer's age.

Identification. The method for identifying a minor is the same as that for an adult. However, determining the identity of a minor can be a problem, because minors often do not possess acceptable identification documents such as driver's licenses or passports. If the minor does not have acceptable ID, then the other methods of identifying acknowledgers must be used, either the Notary's personal knowledge of the minor or the oath of a credible identifying witness who can identify the minor. (See "Credible Identifying Witness," page 11.) ■

Reviewing the Document

Blank or Incomplete Documents

Do Not Notarize. While Michigan does not prohibit notarizing blank or incomplete documents, this is a dangerous, unbusinesslike practice and a breach of common sense, similar to signing a blank check.

A fraudulent document could readily be created above a Notary's signed and sealed certificate on an otherwise blank paper. And, with documents containing blanks to be filled in after the notarization by a person other than the signer, there is a danger that the information inserted will be contrary to the wishes of the signer.

Blanks in a document should be filled in by the signer prior to notarization. If the blanks are inapplicable and intended to be left unfilled, the signer should line through each space or write "Not Applicable" or "N/A." The Notary may not, however, tell the signer what to write in the blanks. If the signer is unsure on how to fill in the blanks, he or she should contact the document's issuer, its eventual recipient, or an attorney.

Photocopies & Faxes

Original Signature. A photocopy or fax may be notarized as long as the signature on it is original, meaning that the photocopy or fax must have been signed with pen and ink. Signatures on documents presented for notarization must always be signed with a handwritten, original signature. A photocopied or faxed signature may never be notarized.

Note that public recorders sometimes will not accept notarized photocopies or faxes, because the text of the document may be too faint to adequately reproduce in microfilming.

REVIEWING THE DOCUMENT

False Documents

Notary Not Responsible. It is not the duty of the Notary to verify the truthfulness or accuracy of the facts in the text of a document. In fact, Notaries are not even required to read the documents they notarize. The Notary is entitled, though, to quickly scan the instrument to extract important particulars (its title, date and number of pages, for example) to record in an official recordbook.

However, if a Notary happens to discover that a document is false or fraudulent, the Notary, as a responsible public official, has a duty to refuse the notarization and to report the attempted fraud to appropriate authorities.

Disqualifying Interest

Impartiality. Notaries are appointed by the state to be impartial, disinterested witnesses whose screening duties help ensure the integrity of important legal and commercial transactions. Lack of impartiality by a Notary throws doubt on the integrity and lawfulness of any transaction. A Notary must never notarize his or her own signature or notarize a transaction to which the Notary is a party or in which the Notary has a financial or beneficial interest (MCL 55.291[7]).

Financial or Beneficial Interest. A financial or beneficial interest exists when the Notary is individually named as a principal in a financial transaction or when the Notary receives an advantage, right, privilege, property or fee valued in excess of the lawfully prescribed notarial fee.

According to Michigan law, a Notary must not notarize if the Notary is named individually in a transaction as a grantor, grantee, mortgagor, mortgagee, trustor, trustee, beneficiary, vendor, vendee, lessor, lessee or as a party to the transaction in some other capacity. These are also regarded as disqualifying conflicts of interest (MCL 55.291[7]).

Exemptions. Certain persons are exempt from this beneficial and financial interest provision. A Notary who is an agent, employee, insurer, attorney, escrow or lender for a person signing a document may notarize the document without being considered to have a disqualifying financial or beneficial interest. For example, a real estate agent can notarize a document relating to a property transfer even if the agent derives a commission from that transaction (MCL 55.291[11]).

Corporations. A Michigan Notary who is a stockholder, director, officer, employee or agent of a bank or corporation may administer an oath to any other stockholder, director, officer, employee or agent of the bank or corporation. However, a Notary who is a stockholder, director, officer or employee of a bank or corporation may not notarize a document if he or she is named as a party to that document (MCL 55.291[10]).

Relatives. State laws prohibit a Notary from notarizing for a spouse, lineal ancestor, lineal descendant, or sibling including in-laws, steps, or half-relatives (MCL 55.291[8]).

It is often difficult for a Notary to retain impartiality with a close friend or relative. Anyone, for example, is entitled to counsel a parent to sign or not to sign an important document, but such counseling is entirely inappropriate for the impartial Notary.

Family members, even those not specifically prohibited by law, should seek a third party Notary to avoid any question of a disqualifying interest.

Refusal of Services

Discrimination. Notaries should honor all lawful and reasonable requests to notarize. A person's race, age, gender, religion, nationality, ethnicity, lifestyle or political viewpoint is never legitimate cause for refusing to perform a notarial act.

Noncustomers. An employer may limit the services of Notary employees to business-related notarizations during hours of employment and exclude services to the general public. Notary-employees may refuse to notarize for noncustomers if their employer has limited the services of Notary-employees to business-related notarizations during hours of employment and has excluded services to the public.

Penalty. Should a Notary refuse to perform a notarial act when lawfully requested, the Notary may be subject to charges of official misconduct. Such misconduct may subject the Notary to removal from office.

Exception. A Notary may refuse to notarize a document if he or she knows that the document is blatantly fraudulent.

Reasonable Care

<u>Responsibility</u>. As public servants, Notaries must act responsibly and exercise reasonable care in the performance of their official duties. If a Notary fails to do so, he or she may be subject to a civil suit to recover financial damages caused by the Notary's error or omission.

In general, reasonable care is that degree of concern and attentiveness that a person of normal intelligence and responsibility would exhibit. If a Notary can demonstrate to a judge or jury that he or she did everything expected of a reasonable person, the judge or jury is obligated by law to find the Notary blameless and not liable for damages.

Complying with all pertinent laws is the first rule of reasonable care for a Notary. And, if there are no statutory guidelines in a given instance, the Notary should go to extremes to use common sense and prudence.

<u>Records</u>. Although not required by law, a Notary's best proof of having exercised reasonable care is a detailed, accurate journal of notarial acts. Such entries as the serial numbers of ID cards and the signatures of credible identifying witnesses can show that the Notary took steps to positively identify every signer. Possession by the Notary of a well-maintained recordbook can prevent lawsuits that falsely claim the Notary was negligent.

Unauthorized Practice of Law

<u>Do Not Assist in Legal Matters</u>. A Notary may not give legal advice or accept fees for legal advice. As a ministerial official, the nonattorney Notary is generally not permitted to assist other persons in drafting, preparing, selecting, completing or understanding a document or transaction.

The Notary should not fill in the blank spaces in the text of a document for other persons, tell others what documents they need or how to draft them, nor advise others about the legal sufficiency of a document — and especially not for a fee.

A Notary, of course, may fill in the blanks on the portion of any document containing the Notary certificate. As a private individual, a Notary may prepare legal documents that he or she is personally a party to; but the Notary may not then notarize his or her own signature on these same documents.

<u>Do Not Determine Notarial Act</u>. A Notary who is not an attorney may not determine the type of notarial act to perform

or decide which certificate to attach. This is beyond the scope of the Notary's expertise and might be considered the unauthorized practice of law. The Notary should only follow instructions provided by the document, its signer, its issuing or receiving agency or an attorney.

If a document lacks Notary certificate wording, the Notary must ask the signer what type of notarization — acknowledgment, jurat or signature witnessing — is required. The Notary may then type the appropriate notarial wording on the document or attach a preprinted, loose certificate. If the signer does not know what type of notarization is required, the issuing or receiving agency should be contacted. This decision is never to be made by the Notary, unless the Notary is also an attorney.

Exceptions. Specially trained, nonattorney Notaries certified or licensed in a particular field (e.g., real estate, insurance, escrow, etc.) may offer advice or prepare documents related to that field only. Paralegals under the supervision of an attorney may give advice about documents in routine legal matters.

Foreign-Language Documents

Proceed with Caution. Although Michigan law does not directly address the notarization of documents written in a language other than English, there are difficulties and dangers in notarizing a document that the Notary cannot understand.

The foremost danger is that the document may have been misrepresented to the Notary. Ideally, documents in foreign languages should be referred to Notaries who can read these languages; in large cities, such multilingual Notaries are often found in ethnic neighborhoods or in foreign consulates.

If a Notary chooses to notarize a document that he or she cannot read, then the Notary certificate should be in English or in a language the Notary can read, and the signature being notarized should be written in characters the Notary is familiar with.

Immigration

Do Not Give Advice. Nonattorney Notaries may never advise others on the subject of immigration, nor help others prepare immigration documents — especially not for a fee. Notaries who offer immigration advice to others may be subject to penalties for the unauthorized practice of law.

Documents. Certain immigration documents may be notarized. Affidavits issued or accepted by the U.S. Citizenship and Immigration Services (USCIS) are most often notarized, with the "Affidavit of Support" (Form I-134) being the most common.

Non-USCIS-issued documents are often notarized and submitted in support of an immigration petition. These may include translator's declarations, statements from employers and banks and affidavits of relationship.

Wills

Do Not Offer Advice. A Notary risks prosecution for the unauthorized practice of law in advising a signer how to proceed with a will. Ill-informed advice may adversely affect the affairs of the signer. The format of a will is dictated by strict laws, and any deviation may result in nullification. In some cases, holographic (handwritten) wills have actually been voided by notarization.

Living Wills. Documents popularly called "living wills" may be notarized. These are not actual wills but written statements of a signer's wishes concerning medical treatment in the event he or she is unable to issue instructions on his or her own behalf.

Special Circumstances. In some states, self-proving wills may require the signatures of the witnesses to be notarized. A Notary should notarize a document described as a will *only* if a Notary certificate is provided or stipulated for each signer, and the signers are not asking questions about how to proceed. Any such questions should be answered by an attorney.

Authentication

Documents Sent Out of State. Documents notarized in Michigan and sent to other states or nations may be required to bear proof that the Notary's signature and seal are genuine and that the Notary had authority to act at the time of notarization. This process of proving the genuineness of an official signature and seal is called *authentication* or *legalization*.

In Michigan, the proof is in the form of an authenticating certificate attached to the notarized document by either the county clerk's office where the Notary has been appointed or the Department of State (MCL 565.263).

Certificate. These authenticating certificates are known by different names: certificates of authority, certificates of capacity, certificates of authenticity, certificates of prothonotary and "flags."

In sending a notarized document from Michigan to another nation, attachment of an authenticating certificate from the Department of State may be necessary in addition to or in lieu of the county clerk's certificate (MCL 565.263).

Procedure. An individual seeking to obtain an authentication certificate through the mail should include a cover letter with the name, address and telephone number of the person making the request.

Contact either the specific clerk of the county in which the Notary has filed an oath and bond or one of the Department of State offices at:

>Regular Mail ($1):
>Office of the Great Seal
>7064 Crowner Drive
>Lansing, MI 48918
>
>Walk-in or Courier Service ($1 plus courier fee and prepaid postage):
>Office of the Great Seal
>Richard H. Austin Building 1st Floor
>430 W. Allegan Street
>Lansing, MI 48915
>Telephone: (888) 767-6424

Depending on the type of mail service requested, issuance of the authentication certificates takes approximately three days to three weeks. Same-day service is available by personally appearing at the second office listed above. No appointment is necessary, but prearrangement is required when requesting certificates for five or more documents. Contact the Department at (517) 373-2531 to prearrange service. If requesting authentication from a county, the individual should visit the office of the county clerk in the particular county.

Documents Sent Out of Country. If the notarized document is going out of the United States, a "chain" authentication process may be necessary. Additional certificates of authority may have to be obtained from the U.S. Department of State in Washington, D.C., a foreign consulate in Washington, D.C. and a ministry of foreign affairs in the particular foreign nation.

Apostilles and the Hague Convention. Fortunately, over 100 nations, including the United States, subscribe to a treaty under the auspices of the Hague Conference. This treaty simplifies authentication of notarized documents exchanged between any of the participating nations. The official name of this treaty, adopted by the Conference on October 5, 1961, is *The Hague Convention Abolishing the Requirement of Legalization for Foreign Public Documents*. For a list of the subscribing countries, visit hcch.net/index_en.php.

Under the Hague Convention, only one authenticating certificate, called an *apostille*, is necessary to ensure acceptance in these subscribing countries. (*Apostille* is French for "notation".) It is not necessary to obtain an authentication certificate from the county prior to requesting an *apostille*.

In Michigan, *apostilles* are issued by the Department of State's office for a $1 fee per authenticating certificate. *Apostilles* are not obtainable from the county clerk.

An *apostille* may be requested in writing by a letter including the name, address and telephone number of the person making the request. The letter must also identify the nation to which the document will be sent. A person requesting the *apostille* should send the letter, the notarized document and the appropriate fee to the Department of State office listed above.

Same-day service is available by personally appearing at the office listed on page 22. No appointment is necessary, but prearrangement is required when requesting *apostilles* for five or more documents. Contact the Department at (517) 335-8656 to prearrange service.

It is *not* the Notary's responsibility to obtain an *apostille* but, rather, it is the responsibility of the party sending the document.

Documents from Other States and Nations. Michigan recognizes the validity of properly authenticated acknowledgments and proofs taken in other U.S. states, territories and districts by Notaries and other authorized officials, including (MCL 565.262):

- A judge, clerk or deputy clerk of a court in the place where the notarization is being performed.

- An officer of the foreign service of the United States or a consular agent.

- A commissioned officer in active service with the Armed Forces of the United States. ■

Official Notary Acts

Authorized Acts

Notaries may perform the following official acts:

- Acknowledgments, certifying that a signer personally appeared before the Notary, was identified by the Notary and acknowledged freely signing the document (MCL 55.263[a] and 55.285[2]). (See pages 26–29.)

- Verifications upon oath or affirmation (jurats), certifying that the signer personally appeared before the Notary, was identified by the Notary, signed in the Notary's presence and took an oath or affirmation from the Notary (MCL 55.265[a], 55.267[d] and 55.285[3]). (See pages 31–33.)

- Oaths and affirmations, which are solemn promises to a Supreme Being (oath) or solemn promises on one's own personal honor (affirmation) (MCL 55.285[1b]). (See pages 33–34.)

- Proofs of Execution, certifying that a subscribing witness personally appeared and swore to the Notary that another person, the principal, signed a document (MCL 565.262). (See pages 34–35.)

- Witnessings or attestations of signatures, certifying that the signer personally appeared before the Notary, was identified and signed in the Notary's presence (MCL 55.285[4]). (See page 36.)

25

Acknowledgments

A Common Notarial Act. Acknowledgments are one of the most common forms of notarization.

Purpose. In executing an acknowledgment, a Notary certifies three things (MCL 565.264):

1) The signer *personally appeared* before the Notary on the date and in the county indicated on the Notary certificate (notarization cannot be based on a telephone call or on a Notary's familiarity with a signature).

2) The signer was *positively identified* by the Notary through either personal knowledge or satisfactory evidence. (See "Identifying Document Signers," pages 10–13).

3) The signer *acknowledged* to the Notary that the signature *was freely made* for the purposes stated in the document and, if the document is signed in a representative capacity, that he or she had proper authority to do so. (If a document is willingly signed in the presence of the Notary, this act can serve just as well as an oral statement of acknowledgment.)

Certificates for Acknowledgment. Upon taking the acknowledgment of any signer, the Notary must complete, sign and seal (if used) an appropriate certificate of acknowledgment. The certificate wording should either be preprinted or typed at the end of the document, or appear as an attachment (a certificate form) that is stapled to the document's signature page.

Michigan law provides "statutory short forms of acknowledgment" which may be used and are sufficient for their purposes under any law of the state. Use of other appropriate forms is not prohibited (MCL 565.267).

- Acknowledgment for an individual acting in his or her own behalf:

    State of Michigan
    County of _____

    The foregoing instrument was acknowledged before me this _____ (date) by _____ (name of person acknowledging).

OFFICIAL NOTARY ACTS

_____ (Signature of Notary)   (Stamp of Notary)

(If not in stamp, print or type Notary's name; "Notary Public, State of Michigan, County of _____;" "My commission expires _____;" if acting in another county other than the county of commissioning, "Acting in the County of _____;" and the date the notarial act was performed.)

- **Acknowledgment for a corporation:**

  State of Michigan
  County of _____

  The foregoing instrument was acknowledged before me this _____ (date) by _____ (name of officer or agent, title of officer or agent) of _____ (name of corporation acknowledging), a _____ (state or place of incorporation) corporation, on behalf of the corporation.

  _____ (Signature of Notary)   (Stamp of Notary)

  (If not in stamp, print or type Notary's name; "Notary Public, State of Michigan, County of _____;" "My commission expires _____;" if acting in another county other than the county of commissioning, "Acting in the County of _____;" and the date the notarial act was performed.)

- **Acknowledgment for a partnership:**

  State of Michigan
  County of _____

  The foregoing instrument was acknowledged before me this _____ (date) by _____ (name of acknowledging partner or agent), partner (or agent) on behalf of _____ (name of partnership), a partnership.

  _____ (Signature of Notary)   (Stamp of Notary)

  (If not in stamp, print or type Notary's name; "Notary Public, State of Michigan, County of _____;" "My commission expires _____;" if acting in another county other than the county of commissioning, "Acting in the County of _____;" and the date the notarial act was performed.)

- **Acknowledgment for an attorney in fact on behalf of an absent principal:**

  State of Michigan
  County of _____
  The foregoing instrument was acknowledged before me this _____ (date) by _____ (name of attorney in fact) as attorney in fact on behalf of _____ (name of principal).

  _____ (Signature of Notary)   (Stamp of Notary)

(If not in stamp, print or type Notary's name; "Notary Public, State of Michigan, County of _____;" "My commission expires _____;" if acting in another county other than the county of commissioning, "Acting in the County of _____;" and the date the notarial act was performed.)

- Acknowledgment for a public officer, trustee or personal representative:

State of Michigan
County of _____

The foregoing instrument was acknowledged before me this _____ (date) by _____ (name and title of position).

_____ (Signature of Notary)   (Stamp of Notary)

(If not in stamp, print or type Notary's name; "Notary Public, State of Michigan, County of _____;" "My commission expires _____;" if acting in another county other than the county of commissioning, "Acting in the County of _____"; and the date the notarial act was performed.)

<u>Alternate Acknowledgment Certificate</u>. Other forms of acknowledgment certificates are acceptable if (MCL 565.265):

- The certificate is in a form prescribed by the laws or regulations of the state of Michigan.

- The certificate is in a form applicable to the place in which the acknowledgment is taken.

- The certificate contains the words "acknowledged before me" or substantially similar wording.

<u>Required Information</u>. Although Michigan law does not require the use of an inking seal or embossing seal, the following information must be typed, printed, stamped or otherwise imprinted mechanically or electronically in a photographically reproducible manner on each Notary certificate (MCL 55.287[2]):

- The Notary's name as it appears on the commission application.

- "Notary Public, State of Michigan, County of _____."

- "My commission expires_____."

- If notarizing in a county other than the county of commissioning, the statement "Acting in the County of _____."

- The date the notarial act was performed.

Identification of Acknowledger. In executing an acknowledgment, the Notary must identify the signer through personal knowledge or another form of satisfactory evidence. (See "Identifying Document Signers," pages 10–13.)

Witnessing Signature. Although Michigan state officials suggest that a document requiring an acknowledgment be signed in the Notary's presence, Michigan law stipulates that a signer must appear before the Notary at the time of notarization to acknowledge having signed the document (MCL 565.264).

In most states, a document could be signed an hour before, a week before, a year before, etc. — as long as the signer appears before the Notary with the signed document at the time of notarization to admit that the signature is his or her own. (However, for a jurat notarization, which requires an oath or affirmation, the document must indeed be signed in the presence of the Notary. See "Jurats," pages 31–33.)

Terminology. In discussing acknowledgments, it is important to use proper terminology. A Notary takes or executes an acknowledgment, while a signer makes or gives an acknowledgment.

Fees. A Notary may charge up to $10 for taking an acknowledgment (MCL 55.285[7]).

Depositions and Affidavits

Purpose. A deposition is a signed transcript of the signer's oral statements taken down for use in a judicial proceeding. The deposition signer is called the deponent.

An affidavit is a signed statement made under oath or affirmation by a person called an affiant, and it may be used for a variety of purposes both in and out of court.

To notarize a deposition or an affidavit, the Notary must administer an oath or affirmation and complete a Notary certificate, which the Notary signs and seals.

MICHIGAN NOTARY PRIMER

Depositions. With a deposition, both sides in a lawsuit or court case typically have the opportunity to cross-examine the deponent. Questions and answers are transcribed into a written statement. Used only in judicial proceedings, a deposition is then signed and sworn to before an oath-administering official.

Michigan law does not empower Notaries to take depositions — meaning, to transcribe the words spoken aloud by a deponent — but Notaries may execute jurats on depositions (MCL 55.285[3]).

The actual taking of the deposition is most often done by trained and certified shorthand reporters, also known as court reporters. While most Notaries do not have the stenographic skills necessary to transcribe a deponent's words, any Notary is competent to administer an oath (or affirmation) or to execute a jurat for a deposition.

Affidavits. Affidavits are used in and out of court for a variety of purposes, from declaring losses to an insurance company to declaring U.S. citizenship before traveling to a foreign country. An affidavit is a document containing a statement voluntarily signed and sworn to or affirmed before a Notary or other official with oath-administering powers. If used in a judicial proceeding, only one side in the case need participate in the execution of the affidavit, in contrast to the deposition.

The following form is acceptable for an affidavit or sworn statement:

State of Michigan
County of _____

I, _____ (name of affiant) (explanation of who affiant is, followed by affiant's statement).

Signature of Affiant
Printed Name of Affiant

Signed and sworn to before me in _____ County, Michigan, on _____ (month/day), _____ (year).

Notary's
Stamp_____

Notary's
Signature_____

(If not in stamp, print or type Notary's name; "Notary Public, State of Michigan, County of _____;" "My commission expires _____;" if acting in another county other than the county of commissioning, "Acting in the County of _____;" and the date the notarial act was performed.)

Certificate for Depositions and Affidavits. Depositions and affidavits usually require jurat certificates in some form. (See "Jurats," pages 31–33.)

Oath (Affirmation) for Depositions and Affidavits. If no other wording is prescribed in a given instance, a Notary may use the following language in administering an oath (or affirmation) for an affidavit or deposition:

> Do you solemnly swear that the statements in this document are true to the best of your knowledge and belief, so help you God?
>
> (Do you solemnly affirm that the statements in this document are true to the best of your knowledge and belief?)

For both oath and affirmation, the affiant must respond aloud and affirmatively, with "I do" or similar words. State officials suggest that the Notary and the person taking the oath or affirmation raise their right hands when administering the oath or affirmation.

Fees. For a jurat on a deposition or affidavit, a Notary may charge no more than $10 per signature (MCL 55.285[7]).

Verifications Upon Oath or Affirmation (Jurats)

Part of Verification. In notarizing affidavits, depositions and other forms of written verification requiring an oath by the signer, the Notary normally executes a jurat.

Purpose. While the purpose of an acknowledgment is to positively identify a signer, the purpose of verification upon oath or affirmation, also called a jurat, is to compel truthfulness by appealing to the signer's conscience and fear of criminal penalties for perjury.

In executing a jurat, a Notary certifies that (MCL 55.265[a] and 55.285[3]):

1) The signer *personally appeared* before the Notary at the time of notarization on the date and in the county indicated on the Notary certificate.

2) The Notary *positively identified* the signer through either personal knowledge or satisfactory evidence.

3) The Notary *watched the signer sign* the document at the time of notarization.

4) The Notary *administered an oath or affirmation* to the signer.

Certificate for a Verification. A typical verification contains the wording, "Subscribed and sworn to (or affirmed) before me" or similar language. "Subscribed" means "signed," and "before me" means that the signer personally appeared.

When verification wording is not prescribed in a given instance, the following wording may be used:

State of Michigan
County of _____

Subscribed and sworn to (or affirmed) before me in _____ County, Michigan, on _____ (month/day), _____ (year), by _____ (signer).

Notary's   Notary's
Stamp_____   Signature_____

(If not in stamp, print or type Notary's name; "Notary Public, State of Michigan, County of _____;" "My commission expires _____;" if acting in another county other than the county of commissioning, "Acting in the County of _____;" and the date the notarial act was performed.)

Wording for Verification Oath (or Affirmation). If wording is not otherwise prescribed by law, a Michigan Notary may use the following or similar words to administer an oath (or affirmation) in conjunction with a jurat:

> Do you solemnly swear that the statements in this document are true to the best of your knowledge and belief, so help you God?
>
> (Do you solemnly affirm that the statements in this document are true to the best of your knowledge and belief?)

Oath or Affirmation Must Be Administered. A Notary Public does not execute a verification by merely asking a signer whether or not the signature on a document is in fact that of the signer. An oath or affirmation must be administered and the affixation of the signature observed by the Notary.

Fees. A Notary may not charge more than $10 per signature for executing a verification upon oath or affirmation (MCL 55.285[7]).

Oaths and Affirmations

Purpose. An oath is a solemn, spoken pledge to a Supreme Being. An affirmation is a solemn, spoken pledge on one's own personal honor, with no reference to a Supreme Being. Both are usually a promise of truthfulness or fidelity and have the same legal effect.

In taking an oath or affirmation in an official proceeding, a person may be subject to criminal penalties for perjury should he or she fail to be truthful.

An oath or affirmation can be a full-fledged notarial act in its own right, as when giving an oath of office to a public official, or it can be part of the process of notarizing a document (e.g., executing a jurat, or swearing in a credible identifying witness).

A person who objects to taking an oath — pledging to a Supreme Being — may instead be given an affirmation.

Wording for Oath (or Affirmation). If law does not dictate otherwise, a Michigan Notary may use the following or similar words in administering an oath (or affirmation):

- Oath (Affirmation) for affiant (affirmant) signing an affidavit or deponent signing a deposition:

    Do you solemnly swear that the statements in this document are true to the best of your knowledge and belief, so help you God?

    (Do you solemnly affirm that the statements in this document are true to the best of your knowledge and belief?)

- Oath (Affirmation) for credible identifying witness:

    Do you solemnly swear that you know the signer truly is the person he/she claims to be, so help you God?

    (Do you solemnly affirm that you know the signer truly is the person he/she claims to be?)

The person taking the oath or affirmation must respond by repeating these words or answering affirmatively with, "I do," "Yes" or similar words. A nod or grunt is not a clear and sufficient response. If a person is mute and unable to speak, the Notary may rely on written notes to communicate.

Ceremony and Gestures. The Notary is encouraged to lend a sense of ceremony and formality while administrating the oath or affirmation and impress upon the signer the importance of truthfulness. During administration of the oath or affirmation, the Notary and the document signer traditionally raise their right hands. Notaries generally have discretion to use words they feel will most compellingly appeal to the conscience of the person taking the oath or affirmation.

'Artificial Persons' Not Sworn. Only an individual may take an oath (or affirmation). An "artificial person" such as a corporation or a partnership may not take an oath.

Personal Appearance Required. An oath (or affirmation) may not be given over the telephone. The person taking the oath or affirmation must physically appear in front of the Notary. In addition, a Notary may not administer an oath (or affirmation) to himself or herself.

Proof of Execution by Subscribing Witness

Purpose. In executing a proof of execution by subscribing witness, a Notary certifies that the signature of a person who does not appear before the Notary — the principal signer — is genuine and freely made based on the sworn testimony of another person who does appear — the subscribing (signing) witness.

Proofs of execution are used when the principal signer is out of town or otherwise unavailable to appear before a Notary. Due to their high potential for fraudulent abuse, proofs of execution are not universally accepted.

Although literature issued by the Michigan Department of State suggests that a Notary should not accept a signature based on the word of a third party, Michigan law does state that proofs may be performed (MCL 565.262).

However, prudence dictates that proofs only be used as a last resort and never merely because the principal signer prefers not to take the time to personally appear before a Notary.

In Lieu of Acknowledgment. On recordable documents, a proof of execution by a subscribing witness is usually regarded as an acceptable substitute for an acknowledgment.

Subscribing Witness. A subscribing witness is a person who watches a principal sign a document (or who personally takes the principal's acknowledgment) and then subscribes (signs) his or her own name on the document at the principal's request. This witness brings that document to a Notary on the principal's behalf and takes an oath or affirmation from the Notary to the effect that the principal is known to him or her, and did indeed willingly sign (or acknowledge signing) the document and request the witness to also sign the document.

The ideal subscribing witness personally knows the principal signer and has no personal beneficial or financial interest in the document or transaction. It would be foolish of the Notary, for example, to rely on the word of a subscribing witness presenting for notarization a power of attorney that names this very witness as attorney in fact.

Identifying Subscribing Witness. Since the Notary is relying entirely upon the word of the subscribing witness to vouch for an absent signer's identity, willingness and awareness, it is best for subscribing witnesses to be personally known to the Notary.

Certificate for Proof of Execution. Michigan statute does not prescribe a Notary certificate for a proof of execution by a subscribing witness. When wording is not provided, the National Notary Association recommends the following format for a proof of execution by a subscribing witness:

State of Michigan   )
) ss.
County of _____   )

On _____ (date), before me, the undersigned, a Notary Public for the state, personally appeared _____ (subscribing witness's name), personally known to me to be the person whose name is subscribed to the within instrument, as a witness thereto, who, being by me duly sworn, deposes and says that he/she was present and saw _____ (name of principal), the same person described in and whose name is subscribed to the within and annexed instrument in his/her authorized capacity(ies) as a party thereto, execute the same, and that said affiant subscribed his/her name to the within instrument as a witness at the request of _____ (name of principal).

Notary's   Notary's
Stamp_____   Signature_____

(If not in stamp, print or type Notary's name; "Notary Public, State of Michigan, County of _____;" "My commission expires _____;" if acting in another county other than the county of commissioning, "Acting in the County of _____;" and the date the notarial act was performed.)

Witnessing or Attesting of Signatures

Purpose. The act of witnessing or "attesting" a signature is similar to a jurat, except that it does not require the signer to take an oath or affirmation. It is used when establishing the signing date is of major importance.

In witnessing or attesting a signature, the Notary certifies that (MCL 55.285[4-6]):

1) The signer *personally appeared* before the Notary on the date and in the county indicated on the Notary certificate.

2) The signer was *positively identified* by personal knowledge or satisfactory evidence.

3) The signer *signed the document* in the presence of the Notary.

Certificate. Michigan laws do no prescribe certificate wording, however the following wording is recommended:

State of Michigan   )
County of _____   )

Signed or attested before me on _____ (date) by ____ (name of person appearing).

_____ (Signature of Notary)   (Seal of Notary)

_____ (Commission Number and Expiration Date)
_____ (Notary Printed Name)
_____ (County Where Appointed)

Fees for Notarial Services

Maximum Fees. For any notarial act — acknowledgment, jurat, administering an oath or affirmation or witnessing or attesting a signature — a maximum fee of $10 is allowed by Michigan law (MCL 55.285[7]).

Inform Before Notarization. Before performing any notarial act, the Notary must inform the signer of the fees, either through a "conspicuous" sign or through expressly advising the person (MCL 55.285[7]).

Travel Fees. Michigan law does not set maximum travel fees for Notaries, but it does indicate that the Notary should inform the constituent in advance if a travel fee is going to be charged and the signer should agree to the amount. The Notary should take care to clarify that such travel fee is separate from the actual notarization fee (MCL 55.285[7]).

Overcharging. Charging more than the legally prescribed fees may subject the Notary to:

- Denial, suspension or revocation of the Notary commission.

- A fine of not more than $1,000.

- A letter of censure.

- A requirement to pay restitution to an injured person or to take other affirmative action.

- A requirement to reimburse the Secretary of State for the costs of the investigation (MCL 55.300a[1][f]).

Advertising Practices

False or Misleading Advertising. The use of false or misleading advertising by a Notary to represent that he or she has duties, rights and privileges not given by law may subject the Notary to charges of official misconduct and removal from office (MCL 55.291[3]).

Translation of "Notary Public". The nonattorney Notary is prohibited from using the literal translation from English into another language of such terms as Notary Public, Notary, licensed, attorney, lawyer or any other term that implies the person is an attorney. This applies to any document, advertisement, stationery, letterhead, business card or any other material describing the role of the Notary Public (MCL 55.291[4]).

Foreign-Language Advertising. If a nonattorney Notary advertises notarial services in a language other than English, the Notary must also display the following prominently in the same language as the advertisement the statement: "I am not an attorney and have no authority to give advice on immigration or other legal matters." The Notary fees as specified by statute must also be included (MCL 55.291[5]).

"Notario Publico". Notaries are prohibited from using the term *"Notario Publico"* or any equivalent non-English term in any business card, advertisement, notice or sign (MCL 55. 291[6]).

Unauthorized Acts

Certified Copies. A certified copy is a verified exact duplicate of an original document. A Michigan Notary is not expressly authorized by law to issue certified copies.

Requests for certified copies should be directed to the agency that holds or issued the original. For certified copies of birth, death or marriage certificates, and other vital records, the person requesting the copy should be referred to the Bureau of Vital Statistics (or the equivalent) in the state where the event occurred.

In states that do not authorize Notaries to certify copies, Notaries may notarize a signed, written declaration made by the owner or holder of a document that a copy is a true copy of the original. This process is commonly called "copy certification by document custodian" and may serve as an acceptable alternative to a Notary-certified copy. The receiving party determines if this alternative is acceptable. The requesting person, not the Notary, should provide the declaration and specify the notarial act to be performed if a Notary certificate is not already provided on the declaration. Notaries should be careful not to guide the process or to make any recommendations or claims concerning the legality or sufficiency of this alternative.

Marriages. Michigan Notaries have no authority to perform marriages unless they are also ministers. Only Notaries in Florida, Maine, Nevada and South Carolina are empowered to perform marriages strictly by virtue of holding a Notary commission. ■

Recordkeeping

Journal of Notarial Acts

Recommended. Michigan law does not directly address the requirement of maintaining a journal. However, state officials strongly recommend that each time a Notary performs a notarial act, he or she should record the signer's name, identification, date of notarization and any additional pertinent information in a recordbook.

Of course, the National Notary Association and many Notary-regulating officials across the nation strongly endorse the policy of keeping a journal of all notarial acts as both protection for the public and the Notary.

Prudent Notaries keep detailed and accurate journals of their notarial acts for many reasons:

- Keeping records is a *businesslike practice* that every conscientious businessperson and public official should engage in. Not keeping records of important transactions, whether private or public, is risky.

- A Notary's recordbook *protects the public's rights* to valuable property and to due process by providing documentary evidence in the event a document is lost or altered, or if a transaction is later challenged.

- In the event of a civil lawsuit alleging that the Notary's negligence or misconduct caused the plaintiff serious financial harm, a detailed journal of notarial acts can *protect the Notary* by showing that reasonable care was used to identify a signer. It would be difficult to contend that the Notary did not bother to identify a signer if the Notary's journal contains a detailed description of the ID cards that the signer presented.

- Since civil lawsuits arising from a contested notarial act typically take place three to six years after the act occurs, the Notary normally cannot accurately testify in court about the particulars of a notarization without a journal to *aid the Notary's memory.*

- Journals of notarial acts *prevent or abort baseless lawsuits* by showing that a Notary did use reasonable care, or that a transaction did occur as recorded. Journal fingerprints and signatures are especially effective in defeating such groundless suits.

- Requiring each signer to leave a signature, or even a fingerprint, in the Notary's journal both *deters attempted forgeries* and provides strong evidence for a conviction should a forgery occur.

Journal Entries. The Notary's recordbook should contain the following information for each notarial act performed:

1) The date, time of day and type of notarization (e.g., jurat, acknowledgment, etc.).

2) The type (or title) of document notarized (e.g., deed of trust, affidavit of support, etc.), including the number of pages and the date of the document.

3) The signature, address and printed name of each signer and witness.

4) A statement as to how the signer's identity was confirmed. (If the signer is personally known, the Notary should indicate that in the journal. If the signer is identified using an ID document, the Notary should record the document's issuer, type, serial number, and date of issuance or expiration. If the signer is identified by a credible identifying witness, the Notary should record the witness's printed name and address and have the witness sign the journal.)

RECORDKEEPING

5) Any other pertinent information, including the fee charged for the notarial service, the capacity of the signer (e.g., president of XYZ Company) or any other significant peculiarities relating to the signer or the document.

Document Dates. If the document has a specific date on it, the Notary should record that date in the journal of notarial acts. Often the only date on a document is the date of the signature that is being notarized. If the signature is undated, however, the document may have no date on it at all. In that case, the Notary should record "no date" or "undated" in the journal.

For acknowledgments, the date the document was signed must either precede or be the same as the date of the notarization; it may not follow it. For a jurat, the date the document was signed and the date of the notarization must be the same.

A document whose signature is dated after the date on its Notary certificate risks rejection by a recorder, who may question how the document could have been notarized before it was signed.

Journal Signature. Perhaps the most important entry to obtain is the signer's signature. A journal signature protects the Notary against claims that a signer did not appear and is a deterrent to forgery, because it provides evidence of the signer's identity and appearance before the Notary. To check for possible forgery, the Notary should compare the signature that the person leaves in the journal of notarial acts with the signatures on the document and on the IDs. The signatures should be at least reasonably similar.

The Notary also should observe the signing of the journal. If the signer appears to be laboring over the journal signature, this may be an indication of forgery in progress.

Journal Thumbprint. Many Notaries are asking signers to leave a thumbprint in the journal. The journal thumbprint protects the Notary against claims that a signer did not appear and is a strong deterrent to forgery, because it represents absolute proof of the signer's identity and appearance before the Notary. Provided the signer is willing, nothing prevents a Notary from asking for a thumbprint for every notarial act. Since a thumbprint is not required by law, however, the Notary may not refuse to notarize if the signer declines to leave one.

Complete Entry Before Certificate. The prudent Notary completes the journal or recordbook entry before filling out the Notary certificate on a document. This prevents the signer from suddenly leaving with the notarized document before vital information can be entered in the journal or recordbook.

Never Surrender Journal. Notaries should never surrender control of their journals to anyone, unless expressly subpoenaed by a court order. Even when an employer has paid for the Notary's official journal and seal, they go with the Notary upon termination of employment. No person but the Notary may properly possess and use these records.

Responding to Secretary's Request to Inspect. Within 15 days after receiving a written or electronic request from the Michigan Secretary of State, the Notary must allow inspection or provide pertinent copies of his or her journal — and keep this information accessible for at least five years after the date of the last notarial act (MCL 55.295).

For failure to respond to such a request, the Secretary may indefinitely suspend the Notary's commission (MCL 55.295[2]). ■

Notary Certificate and Seal

Notary Certificate

Requirement. In notarizing any document, a Notary must complete a Notary certificate. The certificate is wording that indicates exactly what the Notary has certified or attested to. The Notary certificate may be either preprinted or typed on the document itself or added as an attachment to it. The certificate should contain:

1) A *venue* indicating where the notarization is being performed. "State of Michigan, County of _____," is the typical venue wording, with the county name inserted in the blank. The letters "SS." or "SCT." sometimes appear after the venue; they abbreviate the traditional Latin word scilicet, meaning "in particular" or "namely."

2) A *statement of particulars* which indicates what the notarization has attested. An acknowledgment certificate might include such wording as: "On _____ (date) before me, _____ (name of Notary), personally appeared, _____ (name of signer), personally known to me (or proved to me on the basis of satisfactory evidence) to be the person(s) ..." A jurat certificate would include such wording as: "Subscribed and sworn to (or affirmed) before me this _____ (date) by _____ (name of signer)."

3) A *testimonium clause*, which may be optional if the date is included in the statement of particulars: "Witness my hand and official seal, this the ____ day of _____ (month), ____ (year)." In this short sentence, the Notary formally

attests to the truthfulness of the preceding facts in the certificate. "Hand" means signature.

4) The *official signature of the Notary*, exactly as the name appears on the Notary's commission application.

5) The *seal of the Notary*, although not required by Michigan law. An inking seal should be placed near but not over the the Notary's signature.

6) Additional information may be required if it is not included in the Notary seal. Michigan requires the Notary to type, print or stamp the Notary's name, title ("Notary Public") and commission expiration date, the name of the state and county in which the Notary is commissioned, the date the notarial act was performed and, if notarizing in a county other than the county of commissioning, the name of the county in which the notarial act was performed (MCL 55.287).

Completing the Certificate. When filling in the blanks in the Notary certificate, Notaries should either type or print neatly in dark ink.

It is not necessary to select or cross out variable terms such as "he/she/they", "is/are" or a plural "(s)".

Correcting a Certificate. When filling out the certificate, the Notary needs to make sure any preprinted information is accurate. For example, the venue — the state and county in which the notarial act is taking place — may have been filled in prior to the notarization. If the preprinted venue is incorrect, the Notary must line through the incorrect state and/or county, write in the proper site of the notarization, and initial and date the change.

Certificate Forms. When certificate wording is not preprinted on the document, or when preprinted wording is not acceptable, the Notary may attach a certificate form. This form typically is stapled to the document's left margin following the signature page.

If the certificate form is replacing unacceptable preprinted wording, the Notary should line through the preprinted wording and write below it, "See attached certificate." If the document has no preprinted wording, however, the Notary should not add this notation. Those words could be viewed as an unauthorized change to the document.

NOTARY CERTIFICATE AND SEAL

To prevent a certificate form from being removed and fraudulently placed on another document, the Notary may add a brief description of the document to the certificate: "This certificate is attached to a _____ (title or type of document), dated _____ (date), of _____ (number) pages, signed by _____ (name[s] of signer[s])."

The National Notary Association offers certificate forms that have similar wording preprinted on them; otherwise, the Notary will have to print, type, or stamp this information on each certificate form used. Finally, when Notaries attach a certificate form to a document, they always should note in their journals that they did so, as well as the means by which they attached the certificate to the document: "Certificate form stapled to document, following signature page."

While fraud-deterrent steps such as these can make it much more difficult for a certificate form to be removed and misused, there is no absolute protection against its removal and misuse. While a certificate form remains in their control, however, Notaries must absolutely ensure that it is attached only to its intended document.

Selecting Certificates. Nonattorney Notaries should never select Notary certificates for any transaction. It is not the role of the Notary to decide what type of certificate — thus, what type of notarization — a document needs. As ministerial officials, Notaries generally follow instructions and fill out forms that have been provided for them; they do not issue instructions and decide which forms are appropriate in a given case.

If a document is presented to a Notary without certificate wording and if the signer doesn't know what type of notarization is appropriate, the signer should be asked to find out what kind of notarization and certificate are needed. Usually, the agency that issued the document, or that will be accepting the document, can provide this information. A Notary who selects certificates may be subject to the unauthorized practice of law.

Do Not Pre-Sign or Pre-Seal Certificates. A Notary should never sign and/or seal certificates ahead of time or permit other persons to attach Notary certificate forms to documents. A Notary must never give or mail an unattached, signed, and sealed certificate form to another person and trust that person to attach it to a particular document, even if asked to do so by a signer who previously appeared before the Notary. These actions may facilitate fraud or forgery, and they could subject the Notary to lawsuits to recover damages resulting from the Notary's neglect or misconduct.

False Certificates. A Notary who knowingly completes a false Notary certificate may be subject to civil and criminal penalties. A Notary would be completing a false certificate, for example, if he or she signed and sealed an acknowledgment certificate indicating a signer personally appeared when the signer actually did not.

Notary Seal

Optional. Michigan law does not require Notaries to use seals of office, but statutes do stipulate that a Notary must type, print or stamp, in addition to his or her official signature, the Notary's name, title ("Notary Public") and commission expiration date, the name of the state and county in which the Notary is commissioned, the date the notarial act was performed and, if notarizing in a county other than the county of commissioning, the name of the county in which the notarial act was performed (MCL 55.287).

Many Notaries elect to use seals to impart an appropriate sense of ceremony to their official acts. Another very practical reason for using a Notary seal on notarized documents sent to other states and nations: the absence of a seal may delay or, on occasion in foreign nations, prevent the document's acceptance.

Embossing and Inking Seals. There are two types of Notary seals: the traditional metal embossing seal, which crimps its impression onto a paper surface and helps to distinguish photocopies from originals; and the more modern inking stamp, usually with a rubber face, which imprints a photocopiable impression on the paper.

County recording officials prefer inking seals because they considerably simplify the process of microfilming property deeds and other recordable documents. Recorders have to smudge seal embossments with carbon or other photocopiable substances before they can be microfilmed. Michigan law prohibits use of an embossing seal by itself because it is not photocopiable (MCL 55.287[3]).

Required Information. On every Notary certificate, a Notary must type, print or stamp the Notary's name, title ("Notary Public") and commission expiration date, the name of the state and county in which the Notary is commissioned, the date the notarial act was performed and, if notarizing in a county other than the county of commissioning, the name of the county in which the notarial act was performed (MCL 55.287).

Placement of Seal Impression. The Notary's seal impression should be placed near but not over the Notary's signature on the Notary certificate. If there is no room for a seal, the Notary may have no choice but to complete and attach a certificate form that duplicates the notarial wording on the document.

L.S. The letters "L.S." — from the Latin *locus sigilli*, meaning "location of the seal" — appear on many Notary certificates to indicate where the Notary seal should be placed. Only an embossing seal, used in addition to an inking seal, should be placed over these letters. The inking seal should be placed near, but not over, the letters. ∎

Electronic and Remote Online Notarizations

ELECTRONIC AND REMOTE ONLINE NOTARIZATIONS

Uniform Real Property Electronic Recording Act (URPERA)

Michigan signed into law Senate Bill 791, enacting the URPERA, which authorizes county registers of deeds to electronically record electronic real property deeds, mortgages, releases and other documents affecting title to real property. The URPERA also permits a Notary to use an electronic signature in notarizing an electronic real property document without affixing an image of the Notary's official physical seal. In addition, the URPERA creates an Electronic Recording Commission comprised of eight members as specified by the statute to create technical standards for electronic recording in Michigan.

Remote Online Notarization

Michigan Notaries may become an online Notary. Once approved after the application process, an online Notary may notarize documents for any signer through the use of audio-video communication. The same elements of the notarization are still required but the definition of personal appearance has changed to meet the needs of remote online notarizations.

Applying as an Online Notary. A Michigan Notary Public may apply to the Secretary of State to be appointed and commissioned as an online Notary Public. The applicant will need to pay the application fee as well as submit the application electronically to the Secretary of State (Sec. 406.105[a-d]).

Authority to Perform Notarial Acts. A Notary Public may perform a notarial act using a remote online notarization platform if either of the following is met (Sec.26B.5):

— the signer is properly identified and the notarization is completed in same manner as traditional paper notarizations

— the Notary Public is able to identify the document, through a remote online notarization platform, as the same document that was presented by the signer for notarization

Recordkeeping Required. A remote online Notary Public must keep a record of remote online notarizations he or she performs and must maintain only one journal. The journal must be kept as a tangible, permanent bound register or in a tamper-evident, electronic format. The Notary Public must retain the journal for at least 10 years after the performance of the last notarial act recorded in it. The journal must be completed at the time of the notarization and must contain the following entries (at a minimum)(Sec.26B.7-8):

- Date, time and nature of notarial act

- Description of the record, if any

- Full name and address of each individual for whom the notarial act is performed

- Method of identification of signer and the type of ID presented (including issuance and expiration date), if applicable

- Fee charged, if any, for the notarization

The remote online Notary Public must include in the journal a reference to any audio or visual recording performed using a remote online notarization platform and where the recording is stored. The audio or visual recording of the notarial act must be retained for at least ten years after the date of the notarial act (Sec.26B.9).

A Notary Public may designate a custodian to do any of the following (Sec.26B.10):

— maintain the journal that is required for remote online notarizations

— retain the audio or visual recording on his or her behalf (the journal entry should include the custodian's location and contact information)

Identifying Signers Online. A remote online Notary Public must verify the identity of the signer appearing at the time of the notarization through the use of a remote online notarization platform. Their identity may be verified by:

- Personal knowledge of the signer

- Each of the following:

    — Current license, identification card, or record issued by a federal or state government that contains the individual's photograph and signature;

    — Credential analysis; and

    — Identity proofing of the person

    — Credible witnesses personally known to the signer (for credible witnesses not personally known to the Notary, they must show identification) (Sec.25.6]).

Electronic Signature and Seal. The remote online Notary Public must place his or her signature on every record upon which he or she performs a notarial act. He or she must sign their name exactly as his or her name appears on the application for commission as a Notary Public (Sec. 27.1). Signatures are attached to the document through the use of a digital certificat also known as a digital signature. The digital signature is attached to the document in a way that is tamper evident (Michigan E-Notary and Remote Notary Guide 2019). For each notarization, the Notary must print, type, stamp or otherwise imprint mechanically or electronically sufficiently clear and legible to be read by the secretary and must be photographically reproducable. A Notary may use a stamp, seal or electronic process that contains all the information required. (Sec.27.2).

Fees for Online Notarization. A remoteonline Notary Public may charge of fee in an amount not to exceed $10 for performing an online notarization. (Sec.25.7). ■

Misconduct, Fines and Penalties

Prohibited Acts

Misconduct Defined. "Official misconduct" means either exercising power or performing a duty in a way that is unauthorized, unlawful, abusive, negligent, reckless or injurious, or charging more than the maximum authorized by law or both (MCL 55.265[f]).

Liable for Fraud. A Notary found liable for damages resulting from fraud, misrepresentation or other violation is guilty of misconduct (MCL 55.300a[2][e]).

False or Misleading Advertising. The use of false or misleading advertising by a Notary to represent that he or she has duties, rights and privileges not given by law may subject the Notary to charges of official misconduct and removal from office (MCL 55.291[3] and 55.300a[2][f]).

Not Completing Acknowledgment. A Notary who fails to complete an acknowledgment at the time the Notary's seal and signature are affixed may be guilty of misconduct (MCL 55.300a[2][h]).

Not Administering Oath. Failure to administer a required oath or affirmation may be considered misconduct (MCL 55.300a[2][i]).

Unauthorized Practice of Law. A Notary who advises or assists in drafting, preparing or completing legal documents or who offers advice to a signer about how to proceed may be guilty of misconduct (MCL 55.300a[2][j]).

MISCONDUCT, FINES AND PENALTIES

Refuse Request for Records. Hindering or refusing a request by the Secretary of State for notarial records or papers is punishable as misconduct (MCL 55.300a[2][m]).

Unfair or Deceptive Practice. A Notary who engages in any practice that is unfair or deceptive, including misrepresenting the duties or responsibilities of a Notary, may be found guilty of misconduct (MCL 55.300a[2][n]).

Permitting Unlawful Use of Seal. A Notary who fails to safeguard the official seal and permits another to use it may be guilty of misconduct (MCL 55.300a[2][p]).

Failure of Duty. Failure to fully and faithfully discharge the duties or responsibilities of a Notary may subject the Notary to charges of official misconduct and removal from office (MCL 55.300a[2][d]).

Certify Copies and Originals. Michigan Notaries are specifically prohibited from certifying that a document is either an original or a copy of another record (MCL 55.291[1]).

Notarize Own Signature. Notaries are not permitted to notarize their own signatures or documents in which they are named. Likewise, Notaries may not take their own depositions or affidavits (MCL 55.291[2]).

Conflict of Interest. A Notary may not perform a notarial act in connection with a transaction if the Notary has a conflict of interest. This prohibits a Notary from notarizing if he or she is named as a grantor, grantee, mortgagor, mortgagee, trustor, trustee, beneficiary, vendor, vendee, lessor, lessee or as a party in any capacity to the transaction. A Notary with a direct beneficial or financial interest in a transaction, other than the Notary fee, is also prohibited from notarizing (MCL 55.291[7]).

A Notary is not considered to have a beneficial or financial interest in a transaction where the Notary acts as an agent, employee, insurer, attorney, escrow or lender for a signer (MCL 55.291[10]).

Relatives. Michigan Notaries may not notarize for a spouse, lineal ancestor, lineal descendant, or sibling including in-laws, steps, or half-relatives (MCL 55.291[8]).

Overcharging. A Notary who charges more than the legally prescribed fees is guilty of misconduct (MCL 55.300a[2][g]).

False Acknowledgments. A Notary should ensure that a certificate for an acknowledgment reflects the date the signer actually appeared before the Notary. A certificate that indicates a different date than when the signer actually appeared is considered to be fraudulent.

False Certificate. A Notary who knowingly completes a false certificate may be subject to criminal penalties.

Notary's Own Signature. Notaries are never permitted to notarize their own signatures (MCL 55.291[2][b]).

Telephone Notarizations. State law requires that a signer must personally appear before the Notary, face to face in the same room, at the time of the notarization, not before, not after. Acknowledgments and jurats may not be performed over the telephone (MCL 565.264 and 565.266).

Wills. Notaries may not draft wills nor offer advice concerning a will. A Notary should only notarize a document described as a will if a Notary certificate is provided or stipulated and the would-be testator is not asking questions about how to proceed. Any such questions should be answered only by an attorney. (See "Wills," page 21.)

Undue Influence. Since Notaries are appointed to serve as impartial witnesses, a Notary never attempts to influence a person to execute or not to execute a document or transaction requiring a notarial act by that Notary.

Administrative Penalties

Misconduct. For any act of official misconduct by a Notary, the Department of State may impose any of the following penalties: suspension or revocation of the Notary's commission; denial of an application for appointment; a fine of not more than $1,000; mandatory affirmative action determined by the Secretary, including payment of restitution to an injured person; a letter of censure; and requirement to reimburse the Secretary's office for the cost of the investigation (MCL 55.300a[1]).

Application Misstatement. Substantial and material misstatement or omission of information in the application for a Notary

MISCONDUCT, FINES AND PENALTIES

commission may be reason for the Department of State to return the application to the would-be Notary until correction is made.

Falsely Acting as a Notary. Any person who is not a Notary and who represents himself or herself as a Notary Public and causes harm or damages to a private party may be subject to civil action by the injured party.

Felony Conviction

The Secretary of State will automatically revoke the commission of any Notary upon conviction of a felony in Michigan or of a substantially corresponding violation of another state on the date that the felony conviction or corresponding violation is entered (MCL 55.301[1]).

Complaint and Investigation

Secretary May Investigate. The Secretary of State may investigate a Notary who has allegedly violated or is about to violate a statute or rule. Any individual may file a complaint against the Notary with the Secretary of State in a format containing: the complainant's name, address, telephone number and the complainant's signature; the date the complaint was signed; and a complete statement describing the basis for the complaint and the actual document or a copy of the document involved in the complaint (MCL 55.300).

Notary Must Respond to Request. If a Notary receives a written or electronic request from the Secretary of State requesting information, including a copy of the Notary's records or access to inspect the Notary's records, that Notary must comply within 15 days of receiving the request. Failure to respond may result in suspension of the Notary's commission until he or she does comply (MCL 55.295).

Right to a Hearing. Before the Secretary applies an administrative penalty, the Notary affected will be given notice and an opportunity for a hearing (MCL 55.300a[3]).

Civil Lawsuit

Liability for Damages. A Notary may be subject to civil actions for willful violations, including fraud and dishonesty.

Found Liable for Fraud or Misrepresentation. Being found liable for damages in a suit accusing fraud, misrepresentation or violation of state laws may be reason for the Department of State to charge the Notary with official misconduct and removal from office (MCL 55.300a[2][e]).

A Notary found guilty of such misconduct or negligence may also be subject to a civil lawsuit to recover damages.

Protection for Public. Michigan Notaries are required to hold a surety bond in the amount of $10,000. The bond is intended to protect the public against a Notary's negligence and misconduct (MCL 55.273[2]).

Protection for Notary. In some instances, a civil lawsuit against the Notary may seek financial recovery against any and all of the Notary's personal assets.

Errors and omissions insurance may provide limited protection to the accused Notary, but only for unintentional mistakes made while performing a notarial act. Errors and omissions insurance does not protect the Notary for negligence or intentional misconduct.

Felony

Performing Notarization After Commission Revoked. Anyone found guilty of performing a notarial act after his or her commission was revoked is guilty of a felony and is subject to a fine of up to $3,000, imprisonment for up to five years, or both (MCL 55.301[4]).

Knowingly Violating Notary Public Act in Real Estate Transaction. Anyone found guilty of knowingly violating the Notary Public Act when notarizing a document relating to an interest in real property or a mortgage transaction is guilty of a felony and is subject to a fine of up to $5,000, imprisonment for up to four years, or both (MCL 55.309[1][B]).

Mortgage Fraud. To address the problem of mortgage and real property fraud, Michigan has a 10-year statute of limitations to secure indictments for false pretenses involving real property, mortgage fraud, forgery or uttering and publishing an instrument affecting an interest in real property (MCL 767.24[5]).

Anyone who is found guilty of falsely making, altering or counterfeiting a deed, discharge of mortgage or power of attorney affecting an interest in real property with intent to injure or defraud a person, or who is found guilty of publishing as true a false, forged, altered or counterfeit deed, discharge of mortgage or power of attorney, is guilty of a felony and subject to imprisonment for not more than 14 years (MCL 750.248B and 750.249B).

Finally, Michigan law defines "mortgage lending process" as the process through which a person seeks or obtains a residential mortgage loan, including solicitation, application, or origination, negotiation of terms, third-party provider services, underwriting, signing and closing, and funding of the loan (MCL 750.219D). Documents involved in the mortgage lending process include mortgages and deeds, both routinely acknowledged before Notaries.

Misdemeanor

A person committing violations of the Michigan Notary Public Act for which penalties are not otherwise prescribed may be guilty of a misdemeanor punishable by a fine of not more than $5,000 or by imprisonment for not more than one year or both (MCL 55.309[1]).

Specified Misdemeanors. Notaries convicted of two or more "specified misdemeanors" within a 12-month period while commissioned, or three "specified misdemeanors" within a five-year period regardless of being commissioned, will have their commissions revoked by the Secretary of State (MCL 55.301[2]).

The legislation further defines "specified misdemeanors" as misdemeanors which the Secretary determines:

- Violates the Notary Public Act

- Violates the public trust

- Is an act of official misconduct, dishonesty, fraud or deceit

- Is an act substantially related to the duties or responsibilities of a Notary

Reporting Convictions

A commissioned Notary convicted of a felony or misdemeanor in any court must notify the Secretary of State of the conviction in writing within 10 days of the date of conviction (MCL 55.301[7]). ∎

Michigan Laws Pertaining to Notaries Public

Reprinted on the following pages are pertinent sections of Michigan statutes affecting Notaries and notarial acts, mostly drawn from the Michigan Compiled Laws.

MICHIGAN STATUTES

MICHIGAN COMPILED LAWS

MICHIGAN COMPILED LAWS
CHAPTER 55. NOTARIES PUBLIC
MICHIGAN NOTARY PUBLIC ACT

Act 238 of 2003

AN ACT to provide for the qualification, appointment, and regulation of notaries; to provide for the levy, assessment, and collection of certain service charges and fees and to provide for their disposition; to create certain funds for certain purposes; to provide for liability for certain persons; to provide for the admissibility of certain evidence; to prescribe powers and duties of certain state agencies and local officers; to provide for remedies and penalties; and to repeal acts and parts of acts.

History: 2003, Act 238, Eff. Apr. 1, 2004

The People of the State of Michigan enact:

55.261 Short title.
Sec. 1.
This act shall be known and may be cited as the "Michigan notary public act". History: 2003, Act 238, Eff. Apr. 1, 2004

55.263 Definitions; A to I.
Sec. 3.
As used in this act:
(a) "Acknowledgment" means the confirmation by a person in the

presence of a notary public that he or she is placing or has placed his or her signature on a record for the purposes stated in the record and, if the record is signed in a representative capacity, that he or she is placing or has placed his or her signature on the record with the proper authority and in the capacity of the person represented and identified in the record.

(b) "Cancellation" means the nullification of a notary public commission due to an error or defect or because the notary public is no longer entitled to the commission.

(c) "Department" means the department of state.

(d) "Electronic" means that term as defined in the uniform electronic transactions act, 2000 PA 305, MCL 450.831 to 450.849.

(e) "Electronic signature in global and national commerce act" means Public Law 106-229, 114 Stat. 464.

(f) "Information" means that term as defined in the electronic signature in global and national commerce act.

(g) "In a representative capacity" means any of the following:

(i) For and on behalf of a corporation, partnership, trust, association, or other legal entity as an authorized officer, agent, partner, trustee, or other representative of the entity.

(ii) As a public officer, personal representative, guardian, or other representative in the capacity recited in the document.

(iii) As an attorney in fact for a principal.

(iv) In any other capacity as an authorized representative of another person.

(h) "In the presence of" means in compliance with section 101(g) of title I of the electronic signature in global and national commerce act, 15 USC 7001.

History: 2003, Act 238, Eff. Apr. 1, 2004

55.265 Definitions; J to R.

Sec. 5.

As used in this act:

(a) "Jurat" means a certification by a notary public that a signer, whose identity is personally known to the notary public or proven on the basis of satisfactory evidence, has made in the presence of the notary public a voluntary signature and taken an oath or affirmation vouching for the truthfulness of the signed record.

(b) "Lineal ancestor" means an individual in the direct line of ascent including, but not limited to, a parent or grandparent.

(c) "Lineal descendant" means an individual in the direct line of descent including, but not limited to, a child or grandchild.

(d) "Notarial act" means any act that a notary public commissioned in this state is authorized to perform including, but not limited to, the taking of an acknowledgment, the administration of an oath or affirmation, the taking of a verification upon oath or affirmation, and the witnessing or attesting a signature performed in compliance with this act and the uniform recognition of acknowledgments act, 1969 PA 57, MCL 565.261 to 565.270.

(e) "Notify" means to communicate or send a message by a recognized mail, delivery service, or electronic means.

MICHIGAN NOTARY PRIMER

(f) "Official misconduct" means either or both of the following:

(i) The exercise of power or the performance of a duty that is unauthorized, unlawful, abusive, negligent, reckless, or injurious.

(ii) The charging of a fee that exceeds the maximum amount authorized by law.

(g) "Person" means every natural person, corporation, partnership, trust, association, or other legal entity and its legal successors.

(h) "Record" means that term as defined in the uniform electronic transactions act, 2000 PA 305, MCL 450.831 to 450.849.

(i) "Revocation" means the termination of a notary public's commission. History: 2003, Act 238, Eff. Apr. 1, 2004;-- Am. 2006, Act 426, Imd. Eff. Oct. 5, 2006

55.267 Definitions; S to V.

Sec. 7.

As used in this act:

(a) "Secretary" means the secretary of state acting directly or through his or her duly authorized deputies, assistants, and employees.

(b) "Signature" means a person's written or printed name or electronic signature as that term is defined in the uniform electronic transactions act, 2000 PA 305, MCL 450.831 to 450.849, or the person's mark attached to or logically associated with a record including, but not limited to, a contract and executed or adopted by the person with the intent to sign the record.

(c) "Suspension" means the temporary withdrawal of the notary's commission to perform notarial acts during the period of the suspension.

(d) "Verification upon oath or affirmation" means the declaration by oath or affirmation that a statement is true.

History: 2003, Act 238, Eff. Apr. 1, 2004

55.269 Notary public; appointment.

Sec. 9.

(1) The secretary may appoint as a notary public a person who complies with the requirements of this act.

(2) A notary public may reside in, move to, and perform notarial acts anywhere in this state from the date of appointment until the notary's birthday occurring not less than 6 years and not more than 7 years after the date of his or her appointment unless the appointment is canceled, suspended, or revoked by the secretary or by operation of law.

(3) The secretary shall not appoint as a notary public a person who is serving a term of imprisonment in a state correctional facility or jail in this or any other state or in a federal correctional facility. History: 2003, Act 238, Eff. Apr. 1, 2004 55.271 Notary public; qualifications.

Sec. 11.

(1) The secretary may appoint as a notary public a person who applies to the secretary and meets all of the following qualifications:

(a) Is at least 18 years of age.

(b) Is a resident of this state or maintains a principal place of business in this state.

MICHIGAN LAWS PERTAINING TO NOTARIES PUBLIC

(c) Reads and writes in the English language.

(d) Is free of any felony convictions, misdemeanor convictions, and violations as described in section 41.

(e) For a person who does not reside in the state of Michigan, demonstrates that his or her principal place of business is located in the county in which he or she requests appointment and indicates that he or she is engaged in an activity in which he or she is likely to be required to perform notarial acts as that word is defined in section 2 of the uniform recognition of acknowledgments act, 1969 PA 57, MCL 565.262.

(f) If applicable, has filed with the county clerk of his or her county of residence or expected appointment a proper surety bond and an oath taken as prescribed by the constitution in a format acceptable to the secretary. The requirement of filing a bond does not apply to an applicant that demonstrates, in a manner acceptable to the secretary, licensure as an attorney at law in this state.

(2) The secretary shall, on a monthly basis, notify the county clerk's office of the appointment of any notaries. History: 2003, Act 238, Eff. Apr. 1, 2004;-- Am. 2006, Act 426, Imd. Eff. Oct. 5, 2006;-- Am. 2006, Act 510, Eff. Apr. 1, 2007

55.273 Filing; oath; bond; fee.

Sec. 13.

(1) Within 90 days before filing an application for a notary public appointment, a person shall file with the county clerk of his or her residence or expected appointment a proper surety bond and an oath taken as prescribed by the constitution.

(2) The bond shall be in the sum of $10,000.00 with good and sufficient surety by a surety licensed to do business in this state. The bond shall be conditioned upon indemnifying or reimbursing a person, financing agency, or governmental agency for monetary loss caused through the official misconduct of the notary public in the performance of a notarial act. The surety is required to indemnify or reimburse only after a judgment based on official misconduct has been entered in a court of competent jurisdiction against the notary public. The aggregate liability of the surety shall not exceed the sum of the bond. The surety on the bond may cancel the bond 60 days after

Revised 6/24/2016

the surety notifies the notary, the secretary, and the county clerk of the cancellation. The surety is not liable for a breach of a condition occurring after the effective date of the cancellation. The county clerk shall not accept the personal assets of an applicant as security for a surety bond under this act.

(3) Each person who files an oath and, if applicable, a bond with a county clerk as required in subsection (1) shall pay a $10.00 filing fee to the county clerk. Upon receipt of the filing fee, the county clerk shall give an oath certificate of filing and a bond, if applicable, to the person as prescribed by the secretary. A charter county with a population of more than 2,000,000 may impose by ordinance a fee for the county clerk's

services different than the amount prescribed by this subsection. Two dollars of each fee collected under this subsection shall be deposited into the notary education and training fund established in section 17 on a schedule determined by the secretary.

History: 2003, Act 238, Eff. Apr. 1, 2004;-- Am. 2006, Act 426, Imd. Eff. Oct. 5, 2006;-- Am. 2006, Act 510, Eff. Apr. 1, 2007

55.275 Application; format; fee; use of L.E.I.N. provided in C.J.I.S. policy council act; certificate of appointment.

Sec. 15.

(1) An individual shall apply to the secretary for appointment as a notary public in a format as prescribed by the secretary. An application for appointment as a notary public must include the handwritten signature of the applicant and all of the follinging information:

(a) The applicant's name, residence address, business address, date of birth, and residence and business telephone numbers and electronic mail address.

(b) The applicant's driver license or state personal identification card number.

(c) A validated copy of the filing of the bond, if applicable, and oath certificate received from the county clerk.

(d) If applicable, a statement showing whether the applicant has previously applied for an appointment as a notary public in this or any other state, the result of the application, and whether the applicant has ever been the holder of a notary public appointment that was revoked, suspended, or canceled in this or any other state.

(e) A statement describing the date and circumstances of any felony or misdemeanor conviction of the applicant during the preceding 10 years.

(f) A declaration that the applicant is a citizen of the United States or, if not a citizen of the United States, proof of the applicant's legal presence in this country.

(g) An affirmation by the applicant that the application is correct, that the applicant has read this act, and that the applicant will perform his or her notarial acts faithfully.

(h) Any other information required by the secretary.

(2) In addition to the requirements under subsection (1), the secretary may request that an applicant provide a criminal history check and crimincal records check through the Department of State Police according to the procedures established by that department, to check the criminal background of the applicant. The actual cost of any criminal history check or criminal records check is the responbility of the applicant.

(3) Each application shall be accompanied by an application processing fee of $10.00. The secretary shall deposit $1.00 of each fee collected under this subsection into the notary education and training fund established in section 17 on a schedule determined by the secretary.

(4) When he or she receives an application that is accompanied by the prescribed processing fee, the secretary may inquire as to the qualifications of the applicant and shall determine whether the applicant meets the

qualifications for appointment as a Notary Public under this act. To assist in deciding whether the applicant is qualified, if the secretary has not requested that the applicant provide a criminal history or records check subsection (2),the secretary may use the law enforcement information network as provided in the C.J.I.S. policy council act, 1974 PA 163, MCL 28.211 to 28.215, to check the criminal background of the applicant.

(5) After approval of an application for appointment as a Notary Public, the secretary shall mail directly to the applicant the certificate of appointment as a notary public. Each certificate of appointment shall identify the individual as a notary public of this state and shall specify the term and county of his or her commission. History: 2003, Act 238, Eff. Apr. 1, 2004;-- Am. 2006, Act 426, Imd. Eff. Oct. 5, 2006;-- Am. 2006, Act 510, Eff. Apr. 1, 2007

55.277 Notary education and training fund.
Sec. 17.

(1) The notary education and training fund is created within the state treasury. Money from fees collected under sections 13(3), 15(2), and 21(4) shall be deposited into the fund.

(2) The state treasurer may receive money or other assets from any source for deposit into the fund. The state treasurer shall direct the investment of the fund. The state treasurer shall credit to the fund interest and earnings from fund investments.

(3) Up to $150,000.00 shall remain in the fund at the close of each fiscal year and shall not lapse to the general fund. Any amount in excess of $150,000.00 shall lapse to the general fund.

(4) The secretary shall expend money from the fund in the form of grants, upon appropriation, for the purposes of providing education and training programs for county clerks and their staffs including, but not limited to, notary responsibilities, election worker training, and election processes. The secretary shall consult with the president of the Michigan association of county clerks, or his or her designee, when approving grant applications under this section.

(5) The secretary shall annually file a report regarding the balance of the fund at the time of the report and a detailed account of the expenditures in the preceding fiscal year. This report shall be sent to the speaker of the house of representatives, the minority leader of the house of representatives, the majority leader of the senate, and the minority leader of the senate.

History: 2003, Act 238, Eff. Apr. 1, 2004;-- Am. 2006, Act 426, Imd. Eff. Oct. 5, 2006

55.279 Reappointment; licensed attorney as notary public; cause for cancellation of appointment.
Sec. 19.

(1) The secretary shall not automatically reappoint a notary public.

(2) A person desiring another notary public appointment may apply

to the secretary, in a format prescribed by the secretary, for an original appointment as a notary public. The application may be submitted not more than 60 days before the expiration of his or her current notary public commission.

(3) In the case of a licensed attorney granted an appointment as a notary public under this act and after the initial application under section 15, the secretary shall send a reappointment application form to the licensed attorney at least 90 days before the expiration of the current notary appointment. The application for reappointment shall contain a certification to be completed by the applicant certifying that he or she is still a member in good standing in the state bar of Michigan. The applicant shall otherwise comply with the requirements for appointment as a notary public as described in section 15.

(4) The secretary shall automatically cancel the notary public commission of any person who makes, draws, utters, or delivers any check, draft, or order for the payment of a processing fee under this act that is not honored by the bank, financial institution, or other depository expected to pay the check, draft, or order for payment upon its first presentation.

History: 2003, Act 238, Eff. Apr. 1, 2004;-- Am. 2006, Act 426, Imd. Eff. Oct. 5, 2006;-- Am. 2006, Act 510, Eff. Apr. 1, 2007

55.281 Corrected notary public commission.
Sec. 21.

(1) A notary public shall immediately apply to the secretary, in a format prescribed by the secretary, for a corrected notary public commission upon the occurrence of any of the following circumstances:

(a) A change in the notary public's name.

(b) A change in the notary public's residence or business address.

(c) The issuance by the secretary of a notary public commission that contains an error in the person's name, birth date, county, or other pertinent information if the error was made on the notary public's application and was used by the secretary to appoint the person as a notary public.

(2) A notary public shall immediately notify both the secretary and the county clerk of his or her appointment, in a format prescribed by the secretary, upon any change in the factual information stated in the notary public's application for appointment.

(3) The secretary shall notify the county clerk of the applicant's appointment when a corrected commission is issued by the secretary.

(4) If a notary public's certificate of appointment becomes lost, mutilated, or illegible, the notary public shall promptly apply to the secretary for the issuance of a duplicate certificate. The application shall be made on a form prescribed by the secretary and be accompanied by a processing fee of $10.00. One dollar of each processing fee collected under this subsection shall be deposited into the notary education and training fund established in section 17.

History: 2003, Act 238, Eff. Apr. 1, 2004;-- Am. 2006, Act 426, Imd. Eff. Oct. 5, 2006

MICHIGAN LAWS PERTAINING TO NOTARIES PUBLIC

55.283 Obtaining and reading state statutes.
Sec. 23.
Before a notary public performs any notarial act, the notary public shall obtain and read a copy of all the current statutes of this state that regulate notarial acts. History: 2003, Act 238, Eff. Apr. 1, 2004

55.285 Performance of notarial acts; scope; verification.
Sec. 25.
(1) A notary public may perform notarial acts that include, but are not limited to, the following:
(a) Taking acknowledgments.
(b) Administering oaths and affirmations.
(c) Witnessing or attesting to a signature.
(2) In taking an acknowledgment, the notary public shall determine, either from personal knowledge or from satisfactory evidence, that the individual in the presence of the notary public and making the acknowledgment is the individual whose signature is on the record.
(3) In taking a verification upon oath or affirmation, the notary public shall determine, either from personal knowledge or from satisfactory evidence, that the individual in the presence of the notary public and making the verification is the individual whose signature is on the record being verified.
(4) In witnessing or attesting to a signature, the notary public shall determine, either from personal knowledge or from satisfactory evidence, that the signature is that of the individual in the presence of the notary public and is the individual named in the record.
(5) In all matters where the notary public takes a verification upon oath or affirmation, or witnesses or attests to a signature, the notary public shall require that the individual sign the record being verified, witnessed, or attested in the presence of the notary public.
(6) A notary public has satisfactory evidence that an individual is the individual whose signature is on a record if that individual is any of the following:
(a) Personally known to the notary public.
(b) Identified upon the oath or affirmation of a credible witness personally known by the notary public and who personally knows the individual.
(c) Identified on the basis of a current license, identification card, or record issued by a federal or state government that contains the individual's photograph and signature.
(d) With regard to a notarial act performed under section 26b, identified and verified through an identity proofing process or services that is part of a remote online notarization platform approved under section 26b(1), and the person presents an identity document described in subdivision (c) that is verified through a credential analysis process or service that is part of a remote online notarization platform approved under section 26b(1).
(7) The fee charged by a notary public for performing a notarial act shall not be more than $10.00 for any individual transaction or notarial

act. A notary public shall either conspicuously display a sign or expressly advise an individual concerning the fee amount to be charged for a notarial act before the notary public performs the act. Before the notary public commences to travel in order to perform a notarial act, the notary public and client may agree concerning a separate travel fee to be charged by the notary public for traveling to perform the notarial act.

(8) A notary public may refuse to perform a notarial act.

(9) The secretary shall prescribe the form that a notary public shall use for a jurat, the taking of an acknowledgment, the administering of an oath or affirmation, the taking of a verification upon an oath or affirmation, the witnessing or attesting to a signature, or any other act that a notary public is authorized to perform in this state.

(10) A county clerk may collect a processing fee of $10.00 for certifying a notarial act of a notary public.

History: 2003, Act 238, Eff. Apr. 1, 2004;-- Am. 2006, Act 426, Imd. Eff. Oct. 5, 2006

Sec.26B.

(1) The secretary and the Department of Technology, Management, and Budget shall review and approve at least 1 remote online notarization platform for the performance of notarial acts in this state. The secretary and the Department of Technology, Management, and Budget may grant approval to additional remote online notarization platforms on an ongoing basis. A Notary Public shall not use a remote online notarization platform that is not approved under this section.

(2) Subject to subsection (3), in considering approval of a remote online notarization platform in this state, the secretary and the Department of Technology, Management, and Budget shall consider the functionality of the remote online notarization platform in performing an identity proofing process or service or credential analysis process or service.

(3) If a remote online notarization platform has been evaluated, and approved or accepted, by a government-sponsored enterprise of the United States, such as the federal home loan mortgage corporation or the government national mortgage association, the remote online notarization platform is considered approved for use in this state unless affirmatively disallowed by the secretary.

(4) The secretary and the Department of Technology, Management, and Budget shall review their standards for approving remote online notarization platforms for use in this state, and whether the number of approved remote online notarization platforms are sufficient, at least every 4 years.

(5) A Notary Public may perform a notarial act using a remote online notarization platform if either of the following is met:

(a) The Notary Public makes all applicable determinations under section 25 according to personal knowledge or satisfactory evidence, performance of the notarial act complies with section 27, and the Notary Public does not violate section 31 in the performance of the notarial act.

(b) The Notary Public, through use of the remote online notarization platform, personal knowledge, or satisfactory evidence, is able to identify the record before the Notary Public as the same record presented by the individual for notarization.

(6) The Notary Public shall not record by audio or visual means a notarial act performed using a remote online notarization platform, unless the Notary Public dislcoses to the person that requested the notarial act that an audio or visual recording is being made and how the recording will be preserved, and the personal consents or has previously consented to the recording. A Notary Public may refuse to conduct a notarial act using a remote online notarization platform if the person that requested the notarial act objects to an audio or visual recording of the notarial act.

(7) A Notary Public performs notarial acts using a remote online notarization platform, the Notary Public must maintain a journal that records, at a minimum, each of those notarial acts. A Notary Public shall maintain only 1 journal for the recording of notarial acts and must keep the journal either as a tangible, permanent bound register or in a tamper-evident, permanent electronic format. A Notary Public shall retain the journal for at least 10 years after the performance of the last notarial act recorded in it. If a Notary Public is not reappointed, or his or her commission is revoked, the former Notary Public shall inform the Secretary of State where the journal is kept or, if directed by the secretary, shall forward the journal to the secretary or a repository designated by the secretary.

(8) A Notary Public shall make an entry in a journal maintained under subsection (7) contemporaneously with performance of the notarial act, and the entry must include, at a minimum, all of the following:

(a) the date, time, and nature of the notarial act.

(b) a description of the record, if any.

(c) the full name and address of each individual for whom the notarial act is performed.

(d) if the identity of the individual for whom the notarial act is performed is based on personal knowledge, a statement to that effect. If the identity of the individual for whom the notarial act is performed is based on satisfactory evidence, a brief description of the method of identification and the identification credential presented, if any, including the date of issuance and expiration for the credential.

(e) The fee charged, if any, by the Notary Public.

(9) An entry made in a journal maintained by a Notary Public under subsection (7) must also reference, but shall not itself contain, any audio or visual recording of a notarial act performed using a remote online notarization platform. Subject to subsection (1), a Notary Public must retain an audio or visual recording of a notarial act for at least 10 years after the performance of the notarial act.

(10) A Notary Public may designate a custodian to do any of the following:

(a) maintain the journal required under subsection (7) on his or her behalf.

(b) retain an audio or visual recording of a notarial act under subsection (9) on his or her behalf. If an audio or visual recording of a notarial act is transferred to a custodian to hold on behalf of the Notary Public, the journal entry must identify the custodian with sufficient information to locate and contact that custodian.

(11) A notarial act performed using a remote online notarization platform under this section that otherwise satisfies the requirements of this act is presumed to satisfy any requirement under this act that a notarial act be performed in the presence of a Notary Public.

(12) As used in this section:

(a) "credential analysis" means a process or service by which a third party affirms the validity of an identity document described in section 25(6)(c) through a review of public and proprietary data sources conducted remotely.

(b) "identity proofing" means a process or service by which a third party provides a Notary Public with a reasonable means to verify the identity of an individual through a review of personal information from public or proprietary data sources conducted remotely.

(c) "remote online notarization platform" means any combination of technology that enables a notary to perform a notarial act remotely; that allows the Notary Public to communicate by sight and sound with the individual for whom he or she is performing the notarial act, and witnesses, if applicable, by means of audio and visual communication; and that includes features to conduct credential analysis and identity proofing.

55.287 Signature of notary public; statements; stamp, seal, or electronic process; effect of illegible statement.

Sec. 27.

(1) A notary public shall place his or her signature on every record upon which he or she performs a notarial act. The notary public shall sign his or her name exactly as his or her name appears on his or her application for commission as a notary public.

(2) On each record that a notary public performs a notarial act and immediately near the notary public's signature, as is practical, the notary public shall print, type, stamp, or otherwise imprint mechanically or electronically sufficiently clear and legible to be read by the secretary and in a manner capable of photographic reproduction all of the following in this format or in a similar format that conveys all of the same information:

(a) The name of the notary public exactly as it appears on his or her application for commission as a notary public.

(b) The statement: "Notary public, State of Michigan, County of _____.".

(c) The statement: "My commission expires _____.".

(d) If performing a notarial act in a county other than the county of commission, the statement: "Acting in the County of _____.".

(e) The date the notarial act was performed.

(f) If applicable, whether the notarial act was performed electronically or performed using a remote online notarization platform under section 26b.

Revised 5/22/2019

(3) A notary public may use a stamp, seal, or electronic process that contains all of the information required by subsection (2). However, the

stamp, seal, or electronic process shall not be used in a manner that renders anything illegible on the record being notarized. An embosser alone or any other method that cannot be reproduced shall not be used.

(4) The illegibility of the statements required in subsection (2) does not affect the validity of the transaction or record that was notarized.

History: 2003, Act 238, Eff. Apr. 1, 2004;-- Am. 2006, Act 155, Imd. Eff. May 26, 2006

55.289 Repealed. 2006, Act 155, Imd. Eff. May 26, 2006. Compiler's Notes: The repealed section pertained to use of notary form.

55.291 Notary public; prohibited conduct.

Sec. 31.

(1) A notary public shall not certify or notarize that a record is either of the following:

(a) An original.

(b) A true copy of another record.

(2) A notary public shall not do any of the following:

(a) Perform a notarial act upon any record executed by himself or herself.

(b) Notarize his or her own signature.

(c) Take his or her own deposition or affidavit.

(3) A notary public shall not claim to have powers, qualifications, rights, or privileges that the office of notary does not provide, including the power to counsel on immigration matters.

(4) A notary public shall not, in any document, advertisement, stationery, letterhead, business card, or other comparable written material describing the role of the notary public, literally translate from English into another language terms or titles including, but not limited to, notary public, notary, licensed, attorney, lawyer, or any other term that implies the person is an attorney.

(5) A notary public who is not a licensed attorney and who advertises notarial services in a language other than English shall include in the document, advertisement, stationery, letterhead, business card, or other comparable written material the following, prominently displayed in the same language:

(a) The statement: "I am not an attorney and have no authority to give advice on immigration or other legal matters".

(b) The fees for notarial acts as specified by statute.

(6) A notary public may not use the term "notario publico" or any equivalent non-English term in any business card, advertisement, notice, or sign.

(7) A notary public shall not perform any notarial act in connection with a transaction if the notary public has a conflict of interest. As used in this subsection, "conflict of interest" means either or both of the following:

(a) The notary public has a direct financial or beneficial interest, other than the notary public fee, in the transaction.

(b) The notary public is named, individually, as a grantor, grantee, mortgagor, mortgagee, trustor, trustee, beneficiary, vendor, vendee, lessor, or lessee or as a party in some other capacity to the transaction.

(8) A notary public shall not perform a notarial act for a spouse, lineal ancestor, lineal descendant, or sibling including in-laws, steps, or half-relatives.

(9) A notary public who is a stockholder, director, officer, or employee of a bank or other corporation may take the acknowledgment of a party to a record executed to or by the corporation, or to administer an oath to any other stockholder, director, officer, employee, or agent of the corporation. A notary public shall not take the acknowledgment of a record by or to a bank or other corporation of which he or she is a stockholder, director, officer, or employee, under circumstances where the notary public is named as a party to the record, either individually or as a representative of the bank or other corporation and the notary public is individually a party to the record.

(10) For purposes of subsection (7), a notary public has no direct financial or beneficial interest in a transaction where the notary public acts in the capacity of an agent, employee, insurer, attorney, escrow, or lender for a person having a direct financial or beneficial interest in the transaction.

History: 2003, Act 238, Eff. Apr. 1, 2004;-- Am. 2006, Act 426, Imd. Eff. Oct. 5, 2006

55.293 Person with physical limitations; signature by notary public.

Sec. 33.

A notary public may sign the name of a person whose physical characteristics limit his or her capacity to sign or make a mark on a record presented for notarization under all of the following conditions:

(a) The notary public is orally, verbally, physically, or through electronic or mechanical means provided by the person and directed by that person to sign that person's name.

(b) The person is in the physical presence of the notary public.

(c) The notary public inscribes beneath the signature:

"Signature affixed pursuant to section 33 of the Michigan notary public act.".

History: 2003, Act 238, Eff. Apr. 1, 2004

55.295 Request by secretary of state; failure to respond.

Sec. 35.

(1) Upon receiving a written or electronic request from the secretary, a notary public shall do all of the following as applicable:

(a) Furnish the secretary with a copy of the notary public's records that relate to the request.

(b) Within 15 days after receiving the request, respond to the secretary with information that relates to the official acts performed by the notary public.

(c) Permit the secretary to inspect his or her notary public records, contracts, or other information that pertains to the official acts of a notary public if those records, contracts, or other information is maintained by the notary public.

(2) Upon presentation to the secretary of satisfactory evidence that a notary public has failed to respond within 15 days or another time period designated under this act to a request of the secretary under subsection (1), the secretary may notify the notary public that his or her notary public commission is suspended indefinitely until he or she provides a satisfactory response to the request.

History: 2003, Act 238, Eff. Apr. 1, 2004;-- Am. 2006, Act 426, Imd. Eff. Oct. 5, 2006

55.297 Misconduct; civil liability; conditions.

Sec. 37.

(1) For the official misconduct of a notary public, the notary public and the sureties on the notary public's surety bond are liable in a civil action for the damages sustained by the persons injured. The employer of a notary public is also liable if both of the following conditions apply:

(a) The notary public was acting within the actual or apparent scope of his or her employment.

(b) The employer had knowledge of and consented to or permitted the official misconduct.

(2) A notary public and the notary public's sureties are not liable for the truth, form, or correctness of the contents of a record upon which the notary public performs a notarial act.

History: 2003, Act 238, Eff. Apr. 1, 2004

55.299 Violations of notary public laws.

Sec. 39.

The secretary may investigate, or cause to be investigated by local authorities, the administration of notary public laws and shall report violations of the notary public laws and rules to the attorney general or prosecuting attorney, or both, for prosecution. History: 2003, Act 238, Eff. Apr. 1, 2004

55.300 Investigation by secretary of state; complaint.

Sec. 40.

(1) The secretary may, on his or her own initiative or in response to a complaint, make a reasonable and necessary investigation within or outside of this state and gather evidence concerning a person who violated, allegedly violated, or is about to violate this act, a rule promulgated under this act, or an order issued under this act or concerning whether a notary public is in compliance with this act, a rule promulgated under this act, or an order issued under this act.

(2) A person may file a complaint against a notary public with the secretary. A complaint shall be made in a format prescribed by the secretary and contain all of the following:

(a) The complainant's name, address, and telephone number.

(b) The complainant's signature and the date the complaint was signed.

(c) A complete statement describing the basis for the complaint.

(d) The actual record that is the basis for the complaint or a copy, photocopy, or other replica of the record.

(3) The secretary may investigate compliance with this act, the rules promulgated under it, or an order issued under it by examination of a notary public's records, contracts, and other pertinent records or information that relate to the official acts of the notary public. History: 2003, Act 238, Eff. Apr. 1, 2004

55.300a Penalties; evidence; notice and hearing; revocation of commission; fine.

Sec. 40a.

(1) An applicant for an appointment or a commissioned notary public who has engaged in conduct prohibited by this act, a rule promulgated under this act, or an order issued under this act is subject to 1 or more of the following penalties, in addition to any criminal penalties otherwise imposed:

(a) Suspension or revocation of his or her certificate of appointment.

(b) Denial of an application for appointment.

(c) A civil fine paid to the department in an amount not to exceed $1,000.00.

(d) A requirement to take the affirmative action determined necessary by the secretary, including payment of restitution to an injured person.

(e) A letter of censure.

(f) A requirement to reimburse the secretary for the costs of the investigation.

(2) The secretary may impose 1 or more of the penalties listed in subsection (1) upon presentation to the secretary of satisfactory evidence that the applicant for an appointment or a commissioned notary public has done 1 or more of the following:

(a) Violated this act, a rule promulgated under this act, or an order issued under this act or assisted others in the violation of this act, a rule promulgated under this act, or an order issued under this act.

(b) Committed an act of official misconduct, dishonesty, fraud, deceit, or of any cause substantially relating to the duties or responsibilities of a notary public or the character or public trust necessary to be a notary public.

(c) Failed to perform his or her notary public duties in accordance with this act, a rule promulgated under this act, or an order issued under this act.

(d) Failed to fully and faithfully discharge a duty or responsibility required of a notary public.

(e) Been found liable in a court of competent jurisdiction for damages in an action grounded in fraud, misrepresentation, or violation of this act.

(f) Represented, implied, or used false or misleading advertising that he or she has duties, rights, or privileges that he or she does not possess by law.

(g) Charged a fee for a notarial act that was more than is allowed under this act.

(h) Failed to complete the notary public's acknowledgment at the time the notary public signed or affixed his or her signature or seal to a record.

(i) Failed to administer an oath or affirmation as required by law.

(j) Engaged in the unauthorized practice of law as determined by a court of competent jurisdiction.

(k) Ceased to maintain his or her residence or principal place of business in this state.

(l) Lacks adequate ability to read and write English.

(m) Hindered or refused a request by the secretary for notary public records or papers.

(n) Engaged in a method, act, or practice that is unfair or deceptive including the making of an untrue statement of a material fact relating to a duty or responsibility of a notary public.

(o) Violated a condition of probation imposed under subsection (1).

(p) Permitted an unlawful use of a notary public's seal.

(q) Failed to maintain good moral character as defined and determined under 1974 PA 381, MCL 338.41 to 338.47.

(3) Before the secretary takes any action under subsection (2), the person affected shall be given notice and an opportunity for a hearing.

(4) If a person holding office as a notary public is sentenced to a term of imprisonment in a state correctional facility or jail in this or any other state or in a federal correctional facility, that person's commission as a notary public is revoked automatically on the day on which the person begins serving the sentence in the jail or correctional facility. If a person's commission as a notary public is revoked because the person begins serving a term of imprisonment and that person performs or attempts to perform a notarial act while imprisoned, that person is not eligible to receive a commission as a notary public for at least 10 years after the person completes his or her term of imprisonment.

(5) Cancellation of a commission is without prejudice to reapplication at any time. A person whose commission is revoked is ineligible for the issuance of a new commission for at least 5 years.

(6) A fine imposed under this act that remains unpaid for more than 180 days may be referred to the department of treasury for collection. The department of treasury may collect the fine by deducting the amount owed from a payroll or tax refund warrant. The secretary may bring an action in a court of competent jurisdiction to recover the amount of a civil fine.

History: 2003, Act 238, Eff. Apr. 1, 2004

55.301 Automatic revocation; violation as felony; notification of conviction.

Sec. 41.

(1) If an individual commissioned as a notary public in this state is convicted of a felony or of a substantially corresponding violation of another state, the secretary shall automatically revoke the notary public commission of that individual on the date that the individual's felony conviction is entered.

(2) If an individual commissioned as a notary public in this state is convicted of 2 or more specified misdemeanors within a 12-month period while commissioned, or of 3 or more specified misdemeanors within a 5-year period regardless of being commissioned, the secretary shall automatically revoke the notary public commission of that individual on the date that the secretary determines the misdemeanor of which the individual

was convicted is a specified misdemeanor. As used in this subsection, "specified misdemeanor" means a misdemeanor that the secretary determines involves any of the following:
(a) A violation of this act.
(b) A violation of the public trust.
(c) An act of official misconduct, dishonesty, fraud, or deceit.
(d) An act substantially related to the duties or responsibilities of a notary public.

(3) If an individual commissioned as a notary public in this state is sentenced to a term of imprisonment in a state correctional facility or jail in this or any other state or in a federal correctional facility, his or her commission as a notary public is revoked automatically on the day on which he or she begins serving the sentence in the jail or correctional facility. If an individual's commission as a notary public is revoked because he or she begins serving a term of imprisonment and he or she performs or attempts to perform a notarial act while imprisoned, he or she is not eligible to receive a commission as a notary public for at least 10 years after he or she completes his or her term of imprisonment.

(4) An individual found guilty of performing a notarial act after his or her commission as a notary public is revoked under this section is guilty of a felony punishable by a fine of not more than $3,000.00 or by imprisonment for not more than 5 years, or both.

(5) An individual, regardless of whether he or she has ever been commissioned as a notary public, who is convicted of a felony is disqualified from being commissioned as a notary public for not less than 10 years after he or she completes his or her sentence for that crime, including any term of imprisonment, parole, or probation, and pays all fines, costs, and assessments. As used in this section, a "felony" means a violation of a penal law of this state, another state, or the United States for which the offender, if convicted, may be punished by death or imprisonment for more than 1 year or an offense expressly designated by law as a felony.

(6) If an individual is convicted of a violation described in subsection (5), the court shall make a determination of whether he or she is a notary. If the individual is a notary, the court shall inform the secretary of the conviction.

(7) If an individual commissioned as a notary public in this state is convicted of any felony or misdemeanor in any court, he or she shall notify the secretary in writing of the conviction within 10 days after the date of that conviction.

History: 2003, Act 238, Eff. Apr. 1, 2004;-- Am. 2012, Act 425, Imd. Eff. Dec. 21, 2012

55.303 Reapplication after revocation; unpaid fine.
Sec. 43.

(1) Cancellation of a commission is without prejudice to reapplication at any time. Except as otherwise provided for in section 41(3), a person whose commission is revoked is ineligible for the issuance of a new commission for at least 5 years.

(2) A fine imposed under this act that remains unpaid for more than 180 days may be referred to the department of treasury for collection. The department of treasury may collect the fine by deducting the amount owed from a payroll or tax refund warrant. The secretary may bring an action in a court of competent jurisdiction to recover the amount of a civil fine.

History: 2003, Act 238, Eff. Apr. 1, 2004

55.305 Injunction or restraining order.

Sec. 45.

(1) Whenever it appears to the secretary that a person has engaged or is about to engage in an act or practice that constitutes or will constitute a violation of this act, a rule promulgated under this act, or an order issued under this act, the attorney general may petition a circuit court for injunctive relief. Upon a proper showing, a circuit court may issue a permanent or temporary injunction or restraining order to enforce the provisions of this act. A party to the action has the right to appeal within 60 days from the date the order or judgment of the court was issued.

(2) The court may order a person subject to an injunction or restraining order provided for in this section to reimburse the secretary for the actual expenses incurred in the investigation related to the petition. The secretary shall refund any amount received as reimbursement should the injunction or restraining order later be dissolved by an appellate court. History: 2003, Act 238, Eff. Apr. 1, 2004

55.307 Presumption.

Sec. 47.

(1) Subject to subsection (2) and in the courts of this state, the certificate of a notary public of official acts performed in the capacity of a notary public, under the seal of office, is presumptive evidence of the facts contained in the certificate except that the certificate is not evidence of a notice of nonacceptance or nonpayment in any case in which a defendant attaches to his or her pleadings an affidavit denying the fact of having received that notice of nonacceptance or nonpayment.

(2) Notwithstanding subsection (1), the court may invalidate any notarial act not performed in compliance with this act.

History: 2003, Act 238, Eff. Apr. 1, 2004;-- Am. 2006, Act 155, Imd. Eff. May 26, 2006

55.309 Violation as misdemeanor or felony; jurisdiction; penalties and remedies as cumulative.

Sec. 49.

(1) Except as otherwise provided for in section 41(4) or as provided by law, a person who violates this act is guilty of 1 of the following:

(a) Except as provided in subdivision (b), a misdemeanor punishable by a fine of not more than $5,000.00 or by imprisonment for not more than 1 year, or both.

(b) If the person knowingly violates this act when notarizing any document relating to an interest in real property or a mortgage transaction, a felony punishable by a fine of not more than $5,000.00 or by imprisonment for not more than 4 years, or both.

(2) An action concerning a fee charged for a notarial act shall be filed in the district court in the place where the notarial act occurred.

(3) The penalties and remedies under this act are cumulative. The bringing of an action or prosecution under this act does not bar an action or prosecution under any other applicable law.

History: 2003, Act 238, Eff. Apr. 1, 2004;-- Am. 2011, Act 204, Eff. Jan. 1, 2012

55.311 Notary fees fund.

Sec. 51.

(1) The notary fees fund is created in the state treasury. Except as otherwise provided in sections 15(2) and 21(4), an application processing fee, duplicate notary public certificate of appointment processing fee, certification processing fee, copying processing fee, reimbursement costs, or administrative fine collected under this act by the secretary shall be deposited by the state treasurer in the notary fees fund and is appropriated to defray the costs incurred by the secretary in administering this act.

(2) A processing or filing fee paid to the secretary or county clerk under this act is not refundable.

History: 2003, Act 238, Eff. Apr. 1, 2004;-- Am. 2006, Act 426, Imd. Eff. Oct. 5, 2006

55.313 Maintenance of records.

Sec. 53.

A person, or the personal representative of a person who is deceased, who both performed a notarial act and created a record of the act performed while commissioned as a notary public under this act shall maintain all the records of that notarial act for at least 5 years after the date of the notarial act.

History: 2003, Act 238, Eff. Apr. 1, 2004;-- Am. 2006, Act 426, Imd. Eff. Oct. 5, 2006

Sec. 54. This act modifies, limits, and supersedes the electronic signatures in global and national commerce act, 15 USC 7001 to 7031, but does not modify, limit, or supersede section 101(c) of that act, 15 USC 7001 (c), or authorize electronic delivery of any of the notices described in section 103(b) of that act, 15 USC 7003(b).

55.315 Rules.

Sec. 55.

The secretary may promulgate rules pursuant to the administrative procedures act of 1969, 1969 PA 306, MCL 24.201 to 24.328, to implement this act. History: 2003, Act 238, Eff. Apr. 1, 2004

CHAPTER 450. CORPORATIONS
UNIFORM ELECTRONIC TRANSACTIONS ACT

450.841 Signature notarized, acknowledged, verified, or made under oath; satisfaction of requirement.
Sec. 11.
If a law requires a signature or record to be notarized, acknowledged, verified, or made under oath, the requirement is satisfied if the electronic signature of the person authorized to perform those acts, together with all other information required to be included by other applicable law, is attached to or logically associated with the signature or record.
History: 2000, Act 305, Imd. Eff. Oct. 16, 2000 .

CHAPTER 565. CONVEYANCE OF REAL PROPERTY UNIFORM RECOGNITION OF ACKNOWLEDGMENTS ACT

Table of Jurisdictions Wherein Act Has Been Adopted. For text of Uniform Act, and variation notes and annotation materials for adopting jurisdictions, see Uniform Laws Annotated Master Edition, Volume 14.

Jurisdiction
Alaska
Arizona
Colorado
Connecticut
Illinois
Kentucky
Maine
Michigan
Nebraska
New Hampshire
North Dakota
Ohio
South Carolina
Virgin Islands
West Virginia
The People of the State of Michigan enact:

565.261. Short title.
Sec. 1. This act shall be known and may be cited as the "Uniform Recognition of Acknowledgments Act".

565.262. Notarial acts, definition; persons performing out of state.
Sec. 2. As used in this act:
(a) "Notarial acts" means acts that the laws of this state authorize notaries public of this state to perform, including the administering of

oaths and affirmations, taking proof of execution and acknowledgments of instruments, and attesting documents. Notarial acts may be performed outside this state for use in this state with the same effect as if performed by a notary public of this state by the following persons authorized pursuant to the laws and regulations of other governments in addition to any other person authorized by the laws of this state:

(i) A notary public authorized to perform notarial acts in the place in which the act is performed.

(ii) A judge, clerk or deputy clerk of any court of record in the place in which the notarial act is performed.

(iii) An officer of the foreign service of the United States, a consular agent or any other person authorized by regulation of the United States department of state to perform notarial acts in the place in which the act is performed.

(iv) A commissioned officer in active service with the armed forces of the United States and any other person authorized by regulation of the armed forces to perform notarial acts if the notarial act is performed for 1 of the following or his dependents:

(A) A merchant seaman of the United States,

(B) A member of the armed forces of the United States

(C) Any other person serving with or accompanying the armed forces of the United States.

(v) Any other person authorized to perform notarial acts in the place in which the act is performed.

(b) "Satisfactory evidence" means evidence upon which reliance is placed upon either of the following:

(i) The sworn word of a credible witness who is personally known to the notary public and who personally knows the signer.

(ii) A current identification card or document issued by a federal or state government that contains the bearer's photograph and signature.

565.263. Authority of officer, authentication.

Sec. 3. (1) If the notarial act is performed by any of the persons described in subdivisions (a) to (d) of section 2, other than a person authorized to perform notarial acts by the laws or regulations of a foreign country, the signature, rank or title and serial number, if any, of the person are sufficient proof of the authority of a holder of that rank or title to perform the act. Further proof of his authority is not required.

(2) If the notarial act is performed by a person authorized by the laws or regulations of a foreign country to perform the act, there is sufficient proof of the authority of that person to act if any of the following exist:

(a) Either a foreign service officer of the United States resident in the country in which the act is performed or a diplomatic or consular officer of the foreign country resident in the United States certifies that a person holding that office is authorized to perform the act.

(b) The official seal of the person performing the notarial act is affixed to the document.

(c) The title and indication of authority to perform notarial acts of the person appears either in a digest of foreign law or in a list customarily used as a source of such information.

(3) If the notarial act is performed by a person other than 1 described in subsections (1) and (2), there is sufficient proof of the authority of that person to act if the clerk of a court of record in the place in which the notarial act is performed certifies to the official character of that person and to his authority to perform the notarial act.

(4) The signature and title of the person performing the act are prima facie evidence that he is a person with the designated title and that the signature is genuine.

565.264. Certificate of person taking acknowledgment.

Sec. 4. The person taking an acknowledgment shall certify that the person acknowledging appeared before him and acknowledged he executed the instrument; and the person acknowledging was known to the person taking the acknowledgment or that the person taking the acknowledgment had satisfactory evidence that the person acknowledging was the person described in and who executed the instrument.

565.265. Form of certificate of acknowledgment.

Sec. 5. The form of a certificate of acknowledgment used by a person whose authority is recognized under section 2 shall be accepted in this state if 1 of the following is true:

(a) The certificate is in a form prescribed by the laws or regulations of this state.

(b) The certificate is in a form prescribed by the laws applicable in the place in which the acknowledgment is taken.

(c) The certificate contains the words "acknowledged before me", or their substantial equivalent.

565.266 Acknowledged before me, meaning.

Sec. 6. The words "acknowledged before me" means:

(a) That the person acknowledging appeared before the person taking the acknowledgment.

(b) That he acknowledged he executed the instrument.

(c) That, in the case of:

(i) A natural person, he executed the instrument for the purposes therein stated.

(ii) A corporation, the officer or agent acknowledged he held the position or title set forth in the instrument and certificate, he signed the instrument on behalf of the corporation by proper authority and the instrument was the act of the corporation for the purpose therein stated.

(iii) A partnership, the partner or agent acknowledged he signed the instrument on behalf of the partnership by proper authority and he executed the instrument as the act of the partnership for the purposes therein stated.

(iv) A person acknowledging as principal by an attorney in fact, he executed the instrument by proper authority as the act of the principal for the purposes therein stated.

(v) A person acknowledging as a public officer, trustee, administrator, guardian or other representative, he signed the instrument by proper authority and he executed the instrument in the capacity and for the purposes therein stated.

(d) That the person taking the acknowledgment either knew or had satisfactory evidence that the person acknowledging was the person named in the instrument or certificate.

565.267. Statutory short forms of acknowledgment.

Sec. 7. (1) The forms of acknowledgment set forth in this section may be used and are sufficient for their purposes under any law of this state. The forms shall be known as "statutory short forms of acknowledgment" and may be referred to by that name. The authorization of the forms in this section does not preclude the use of other forms.

(2) For an individual acting in his own right:

State of _____
County of _____

The foregoing instrument was acknowledged before me this (date) by (name of person acknowledged).

(Signature of person taking acknowledgment)
(Title or rank)
(Serial number, if any)

(3) For a corporation:

State of _____
County of _____

The foregoing instrument was acknowledged before me this (date) by (name of officer or agent, title or officer or agent) of (name of corporation acknowledging) a (state or place of incorporation) corporation, on behalf of the corporation.

(Signature of person taking acknowledgment)
(Title or rank)
(Serial number, if any)

(4) For a partnership:

State of _____
County of _____

The foregoing instrument was acknowledged before me this (date) by (name of acknowledging partner or agent), partner (or agent) on behalf of (name of partnership), a partnership.

(Signature of person taking acknowledgment)
(Title or rank)
(Serial number, if any)

(5) For an individual acting as principal by an attorney in fact:

State of _____
County of _____

The foregoing instrument was acknowledged before me this (date) by (name of attorney in fact) as attorney in fact on behalf of (name of principal).

(Signature of person taking acknowledgment)
(Title or rank)
(Serial number, if any)

(6) By any public officer, trustee or personal representative:

State of _____
County of _____

The foregoing instrument was acknowledged before me this (date) by (name and title of position).

(Signature of person taking acknowledgment)
(Title or rank)
(Serial number, if any)

565.268. Prior notarial acts unaffected.
Sec. 8. A notarial act performed prior to the effective date of this act is not affected by this act. This act provides an additional method of proving notarial acts. Nothing in this act diminishes or invalidates the recognition accorded to notarial acts by other laws of this state.

565.269. Uniform interpretation.
Sec. 9. This act shall be so interpreted as to make uniform the laws of those states which enact it.

565.270. Repealer.
Sec. 10. Act No. 185 of the Public Acts of 1895, 565.256 of the Compiled Laws of 1948, is repealed.

565.8 Deeds; execution; witnesses; acknowledgment; endorsement; validity and legality of certain acknowledgments and recordations of deeds; recorded deed lacking 1 or more witnesses.
Sec. 8. Deeds executed within this state of lands, or any interest in lands, shall be acknowledged before any judge, clerk of a court of record, or notary public within this state. The officer taking the acknowledgment shall endorse on the deed a certificate of the acknowledgment, and the true date of taking the acknowledgment, under his or her hand. Any deed that was acknowledged before any county clerk or clerk of any circuit court, before September 18, 1903, and the acknowledgment of the deed, and, if recorded, the record of the deed, shall be as valid for all purposes so far as the acknowledgment and record are concerned, as if the deed had been

acknowledged before any other officer named in this section, and the legality of the acknowledgment and record shall not be questioned in any court or place. If a deed has been recorded that lacks 1 or more witnesses and the deed has been of record for a period of 10 years or more, and is otherwise eligible to record, the record of the deed shall be effectual for all purposes of a legal record and the record of the deed or a transcript of the record may be given in evidence in all cases and the deed shall be as valid and effectual as if it had been duly executed in compliance with this section.

History: R.S. 1846, Ch. 65;—CL 1857, 2727;—CL 1871, 4210;—How. 5658;—CL 1897, 8962;—Am. 1903, Act 117, Eff. Sept. 15, 1903;—Am. 1905, Act 103, Imd. Eff. May 10, 1905;—CL 1915, 11694;—CL 1929, 13284;—Am. 1937, Act 162, Imd. Eff. July 9, 1937;—CL 1948, 565.8;—Am. 1980, Act 488, Imd. Eff. Jan. 21, 1981;—Am. 2002, Act 23, Imd. Eff. Mar. 4, 2002.

CHAPTER 565. CONVEYANCES OF REAL PROPERTY ACT 123 OF 210. UNIFORM REAL PROPERTY ELECTRONIC RECORDING ACT

565.843 Electronic document or signature; satisfaction of recording requirement; acceptance by register of deeds not required.
Sec. 3.

(1) If a law requires as a condition for recording that a document be an original, be on paper or another tangible medium, or be in writing, the requirement is satisfied by an electronic document.

(2) If a law requires as a condition for recording that a document be signed, the requirement is satisfied by an electronic signature.

(3) A requirement that a document or a signature associated with a document be notarized, acknowledged, verified, witnessed, or made under oath is satisfied if the electronic signature of the person authorized to perform that act, and all other information required to be included, is attached to or logically associated with the document or signature. A physical or electronic image of a stamp, impression, or seal need not accompany an electronic signature.

(4) This section does not require that a register of deeds accept electronic documents for recording.

History: 2010,Act 123, Imd. Eff. July 19, 2010 ■

About the NNA

Since 1957, the National Notary Association has been committed to serving and educating the nation's Notaries. During that time, the NNA® has become known as the most trusted source of information for and about Notaries and Notary laws, rules and best practices.

The NNA serves Notaries through its NationalNotary.org website, social media, publications, annual conferences, seminars, online training and the NNA® Hotline, which offers immediate answers to specific questions about notarization.

In addition, the NNA offers the highest quality professional supplies, including official seals and stamps, recordkeeping journals, Notary certificates and Notary bonds.

Though dedicated primarily to educating and assisting Notaries, the NNA supports implementing effective Notary laws and informing the public about the Notary's vital role in today's society.

To learn more about the National Notary Association, visit NationalNotary.org. ∎

Index

A
Acknowledgment......................26–29
Address change 8
Administrative penalties...........54–55
Advice 19–20
Affidavit....................................29–31
Affirmation..............................33–34
Apostilles....................................23–24
Attesting signatures 36
Authentication........................21–23
Authorized acts........................25–26
Awareness... 9

B
Beneficial interest...........................17
Birth certificates.............................38
Bond..5–6

C
Capacity of signer..........................41
Certificate forms 44–45
Certificates, Notary 43–46
Certified copies..............................38
Commission 3–8
Complaint and investigation..........55
Copy certification by document
    custodian................................38
Credible identifying witness 11–12
Customers 18

D
Death certificates...........................38
Department of State 4

E
Deposition 29–31
Discrimination...............................18
Disqualifying interest...............17–18

E
Electronic and remote online
    notarizations 48–51
Electronic signatures 48–49
Embosser.................................46–47
Errors and omissions insurance...... 6

F
Family members 18
Faxes 16–17
Fees...36–37
Felony 56–57
Felony conviction..........................55
Financial interest.....................17–18
Fines...52–57
Flags 22

H
Hague Convention 23–24

I
Identification...........................10–14
    Satisfactory evidence............10–11
Immigration 20–21

J
Jurat...31–33
Jurisdiction 6

84

INDEX

L
Laws, notarial 58–82
Legalization 21–23
Liability 55

M
Marriages 38
Michigan Compiled Laws
  (MCL) 58–82
Minors 14–15
Misconduct 52–57
Misdemeanor 57–58
Mortgage fraud 56–57

N
Name change 8
Notarial acts 25–38
Notario Publico 38
Notary certificates 43–46
Notary seal 46–47

O
Oath 33–35
Oath of office 6–7

P
Penalties 52–57
Personal knowledge of identity 10
Photocopies 16–17
Prohibited acts 52–54
Proof of execution by subscribing
  witness 34–36
Prothonotary 22

Q
Qualifications 3–4

R
Reasonable care 19
Refusal of services 18
Remote online notarization 48–51
Reporting convictions 57
Residency 3
Resignation 7–8

S
Satisfactory evidence of
  identity 10–11
Seal 46–47
Self-notarization 54
Signature by mark 21–22
Statement of particulars 43
Statutes pertaining to
  notarization 58–82
Subscribing witness 34–36
Surety 5–6

T
Term 7
Testimonium clause 43
Thumbprint 41

U
Unauthorized acts 38–39
Unauthorized practice of law .. 19–20
Uniform Real Property Electronic
  Recording Act (URPERA) 48

V
Venue 43
Verification by jurat 31–33

W
Weddings 38
Willingness 9
Wills 36
Witnessing signatures 36

85

NOTES